A VISUAL, STEP-BY-STEP GUIDE FOR

RE-ENVISIONING RIGOR

Book 2

Powerful Routines for Promoting Rigorous Problem- and Project-Based Learning

Michael McDowell & Aaron Eisberg

Copyrighted Material
A Visual, Step-by-Step Guide for Re-Envisioning Rigor: Powerful Routines for Problem and Project Based Learning

Copyright © 2025 by Michael McDowell & Aaron Eisberg. All Rights Reserved.

No part of this publication may be reproduced, stored in a retrieval system or transmitted, in any form or by any means – electronic, mechanical, photocopy, recording, or otherwise –without prior written permission from the publisher, except for the inclusion of brief quotations in a review.

For more information about this title or to order other books and/or electronic media, contact the publisher:
Mimi and Todd Press
1090 North Palm Canyon Drive
Suite B
Palm Springs, CA 92262
www.mimitoddpress.com

ISBN: 978-1-950089-22-2 (paperback)
ISBN: 978-1-950089-23-9 (epub)

Printed in the United States of America
Program Director: Paul J. Bloomberg
Publishing Manager: Tony Francoeur
Production Editor: Isaac Wells
Development Editor: Dan Alpert
Copy Editor: Terri Lee Paulsen
Layout: Darlene Swanson
Illustrations: Studio Pocketsize
Cover Design: Alison Cox
Indexer: Maria Sosnowski
Office Manager: Leah Tierney

Contents

INTRODUCTION
  The Power of Nuance Through Rigorous Teaching and Learning 3

THE RIGHT HABITS 5
  Habit Placement 6
    Dispositional Strategies Are Universal 7
    Surface, Deep, and Transfer Strategies Are Situational 7
  Habit Mapping 8
    Where Do Strategies Belong? 9
    Moving From Framework to Action 9
  Habit Placement & Sequence in Rigorous PBL by Design 11
    Four-Square Routines Within the Rigorous PBL Methodology 13
  Breaking Rigorous Routines Into Visual Steps 14
  How to Use the Visual Guide 16
  Dashboard & Icons (Left-Hand Page) 16
    How to Use It 16
    Icons & Their Meaning 17
    The First Icon: Impact 17
  The Four-Square Steps (Right-Hand Page) 17
  Using the Guide for Collaborative Professional Learning 18

PHASE 1: PROJECT LAUNCH 22
  Matrix Problems 24
  Clues Approach 26
  Assessment Scramble 28

Know/Need to Know List...30
To and Through...32
Compass Points...34

PHASE 2: SURFACE WORKSHOP..36
Zoom In, Zoom Out...38
Search and Unseen Questions...40
Comparing Work Samples..42
Guided Practice...44
Numberless/Slow Reveal..46
I Describe, You Draw..48

PHASE 3: DEEP WORKSHOP OVERVIEW..50
Venn Diagram..52
2 Box Induction...54
4 A's Protocol..56
SPAR (Spontaneous Argumentation)..58
Frayer Model..60
In2Out Protocol...62

PHASE 4 - PROJECT CONCLUSION AND REFLECTION..................................64
3 C's...66
Jigsaw..68
Red Team..70
Situation Room..72
Friendly Controversy..74
Gallery Walk..76

CONCLUSION..79
References..81
Glossary..83
Index...89

Dedications

For Aaron

From our early conversations to our continued partnership, your insight, creativity, and shared commitment to making project-based learning more accessible, engaging, and rigorous have shaped every chapter of this work. I'm grateful to keep building this vision with you.

-Michael

For my parents, whose example of hard work, grit, and perseverance laid the foundation for who I am. Your steadfast values have shaped every step of my journey and continue to guide me. Your love is always present—steady, strong, and unconditional.

For my brother, whose steady presence and loyalty have been a constant source of strength. You have shown me the power of consistency, trust, and showing up when it matters most.

-Aaron

About the Authors

MICHAEL MCDOWELL, EdD. was a public school educator for eighteen years serving in the roles of classroom teacher, academic and athletic coach, school principal, assistant superintendent of personnel and instruction, and superintendent. During his tenure as a superintendent, his school district received state and national accolades including the National Blue Ribbon Award which recognized their work for student performance and mental health and well-being in the midst of the COVID-19 pandemic by the U.S. Department of Education.

Dr. McDowell serves on numerous boards, served as a college professor, and worked for non-profit organizations to enhance student learning around the world. Over the course of his career, Dr. McDowell has authored bestselling books, created professional learning programs and workbooks, provided keynotes and workshops, and provided practical tools and resources for thousands of teachers and leaders on almost every continent around the world. A prolific author and consultant, Dr. McDowell is recognized as one of the leading authorities on integrating innovative and impactful practices into schools. Offering keynotes and executive coaching to heads of school around the world, he partners with educational leaders to implement high leverage strategies that will enhance teaching and learning in classrooms, schools, and systems.

Bring an author out to your system.
Contact us at info@mimitoddpress.com to get started.

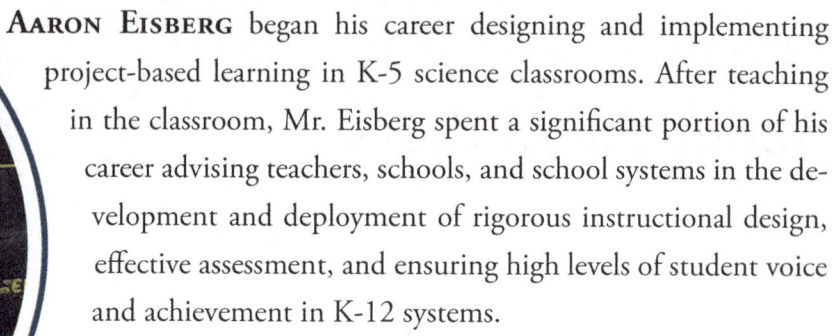

AARON EISBERG began his career designing and implementing project-based learning in K-5 science classrooms. After teaching in the classroom, Mr. Eisberg spent a significant portion of his career advising teachers, schools, and school systems in the development and deployment of rigorous instructional design, effective assessment, and ensuring high levels of student voice and achievement in K-12 systems.

Mr. Eisberg currently works as the Director for the Center for Excellence at New Technology High School, the flagship school of the New Tech Network. As the Director he leads the work of designing new content for faculty, cultivating and curating professional learning for educators around the world, and supporting Napa New Tech High School in strengthening their student-led culture and meeting core academic and 21st Century outcomes. Mr. Eisberg is well regarded in his ability to lead adult professional learning in the utilization of innovative methodologies in today's classrooms.

Concurrently, Mr. Eisberg works closely with Hinge Education to bring forward Rigorous Problem and Project Based Learning and Leadership to school systems around the world. He has worked closely with Dr. McDowell to create and implement the best possible professional learning service to faculty and administration. His focus has always been and continues to be on ensuring students substantially improve in their core academic learning and in developing their efficacy to take ownership over their own learning. Aaron brings an experience and knowledge base in authentic project-based learning juxtaposed with sound research based practices that move students' academic achievement forward. Additionally, Mr. Eisberg is one of the longest standing Buck Institute of Education National Faculty members.

Aaron received a B.S. degree in Natural Science from Loyola Marymount University and a Masters Degree in Elementary Education from Indiana University Bloomington. He holds a Multiple Subject Credential and single subject credentials in Biological Sciences, Introductory Science and Technology.

Bring an author out to your system.
Contact us at info@mimitoddpress.com to get started.

Introduction

Substituting nuance for novelty is what experts do, and that is why they are never bored.
— Angela Duckworth

IN THE REALM OF COMPETITIVE sports, victory often hinges on the smallest of margins. At the Olympic level, a mere fraction of a second can separate gold medalists from those who barely qualify. This principle of marginal gains, where tiny adjustments yield significant results, is not limited to athletics. The slight change in pressure and bending of a guitar string or the slight shifts in speed or tone of a keynote speaker shifts the emotional resonance of a song or story to an audience. Such nuance extends into the realm of education, where subtle shifts in teaching practices can lead to dramatic improvements in student outcomes.

As an example, let's look at lecture versus direct instruction. The learning gains for students equate to a loss of learning of over a year to gaining more than 1.5 years of learning (Hattie, 2023). The impact often comes from teachers who make subtle shifts, such as deploying a particular type of question, timing the question for the right moment, and responding to student responses at the right time (Rosenshine, 2012). For instance, a teacher may subtly shift from asking "Any questions?" at the end of class to "What part of today's lesson felt completely new to you?" The shift may be subtle, yet the impact may be found almost immediately. Students who had never raised their hands before suddenly found their voices. Such practices can unlock a student's potential and drive deeper understanding. Small changes matter in teaching and learning.

Finding this edge is critical in all methodologies, but especially in inquiry-based approaches. Problem- and project-based learning (PBL), which we define as academically rigorous learning that happens in context, is a complex methodology with a checkered past. Rooted in real-world challenges and student-driven inquiry, PBL engages learners in sustained exploration, critical thinking, and authentic problem-solving. While its implementation has varied widely over time, effective PBL remains grounded in meaningful context, high expectations, and purposeful collaboration. The range of impact is equivalent to students regressing more than a year in their learning to demonstrating more than two years of academic growth (Hattie, 2023). Imagine a student group working together to make a slide deck in one room about the dangers of climate change in their local context and in another room a teacher is expecting students to debate the dangers of climate change using claims, evidence, and reasoning that aligns directly with their content standards before making a slide deck. Both rooms may be busy and engaging to students. The subtle demand of using claims, evidence, and reasoning has a high probability of boosting students' argumentative skills and understanding of core content.

These subtleties are often invisible to the casual observer and to practitioners who are not spending time focusing on precise shifts in their work. Our redundancy of practice may lull the crucial moves that are so powerful. As we gain experience in a field, we sometimes lose sight of crucial nuances. Like a long-married couple who finishes each other's sentences, we can become so familiar with our domain that we skip over the subtle variations that once captivated us. The power of nuance lies in its ability to reveal the hidden truths that generalities often obscure. Teachers who look for the edge of their craft, and that of their students' performance, unlock reserved passion for their professional careers and foster growth for their students.

We often suffer this fate when we attend professional learning, yearning for novelty rather than nuance. It's challenging to have the discipline to focus on such fine granularity when new tools, like AI and PBL, are exciting. Interestingly, the hidden impact of our work in the classrooms is in the nuance of our current practices and that of many of our students.

This certainly doesn't mean novelty doesn't matter, but it means we take nuance as seriously as novelty. In his piece, "You Might be a Late Bloomer," David Brooks (2024) argues that late bloomers peak late in their craft because they find new ideas that are hidden by small shifts in their practices. These small shifts release innovation and, often, impact. We need to balance the power of both a range of new ideas, skills, and contexts with the nuanced appreciation of small shifts in practice. One of the small shifts we should consider is how methodologies like PBL can be viewed as a sequence of instructional routines that can be implemented together to form a full problem or project experience for students or could be viewed as a way to deploy one or two habits in a classroom to build students' habits of problem-solving in a traditional class.

The challenge for the reader is to maintain a beginner's perspective, even when confronted with assumptions they deeply value or details they might overlook due to their accumulated expertise. It's about finding the sweet spot between knowledge and curiosity, between confidence and humility. As we approach a methodology like PBL, many of us have past experiences and carry with us stories of "good" and "bad"

INTRODUCTION

projects. We ask that you suspend or hold your assumptions throughout this book and see if you can find nuance rather than scanning for novelty. We ask that you find a willingness to discover new subtleties, to question your assumptions, and to explore the spaces between the generalities we've come to accept as an unloveable truth.

The power of nuance is the power of precision. It's the understanding that in many areas of life, the devil, and the divine, is in the details. By honing our ability to perceive and appreciate these subtleties, we open ourselves to a richer, more textured experience of the world, and unlock new levels of mastery in our chosen pursuits.

This text is about providing teachers and those who support teachers a nuanced approach to teaching inquiry-based approaches. For those of you reading this with years of experience, approach this with a beginner's eye. Think about what's new. What subtle differences do you notice? For those who are new to PBL, consider the small actions that elevate student performance and engagement. What are the small shifts in student behavior?

Problem- and project-based learning is a methodology that both authors hold near and dear to our hearts. The method has a checkered past but holds within it the possibilities of high engagement, innovation, and, yes, academic achievement. This takes small steps, done the right way. This book offers those small steps in a visual manner, providing the edge we need to allow nuance to manifest into novelty for our students and, perhaps, for ourselves.

The Power of Nuance Through Rigorous Teaching and Learning

In 2009, the educational world was rocked by a groundbreaking revelation from Professor John Hattie. Through a meticulous synthesis of research studies spanning virtually every aspect of education and an analysis of data from over a quarter of a million students, Hattie unveiled a startling conclusion: nearly every instructional approach and intervention appeared to yield positive results. This aggregate finding, along with his more recent study in 2023 spanning 400 million students, challenged long-held assumptions and forced educators to reevaluate the very foundations upon which they had built their practices. Hattie's work has ignited a renewed quest to focus on ensuring consistency and precision of the practices that are truly transformative for student learning (Hattie, 2023).

The culminating premise is we need to be much more discerning of what we choose, and what we choose needs to be done with consistency and precision. As Rosenshine (2012) argues, it is the degree to which we engage in a practice, not whether we implement the work. Everyone can try the butterfly, but we only improve upon that stroke if we engage in it every day.

He argued that nuanced approaches to our current practices are the unlocking mechanism to yielding high impact on student learning. He went further to say that searching for novelties, such as new computers and new schedules and new school structures, were minimally successful at best. We need the right routines, done correctly, at the right time.

The Right Habits

The right habits have to do with building students' ability to learn how to learn and how to learn core content. The former is associated with the dispositional habits to navigate learning. The latter is associated with building knowledge, relating ideas, and applying those ideas into other contexts (see Table I.1).

Table 1 Rigorous Learning Descriptions and Examples

Learning Type	Description	Example
Dispositional Learning	Mindsets, attitudes, and behaviors that enable effective learning.	Habits like metacognition, navigating challenges, collaborating with peers, and deliberate practice empower students to embrace challenges, learn from setbacks, and continually strive for mastery across all modes of learning.
Surface Learning	Builds foundational knowledge (facts, vocabulary, procedures). Essential for deeper learning but insufficient on its own.	Understanding U.S. Government Structure – Students memorize the roles of the executive, legislative, and judicial branches, along with key terms like separation of powers and judicial review.
Deep Learning	Focuses on relationships, critical analysis, and meaningful connections between concepts.	Examining Checks and Balances – Students analyze how branches limit each other, study historical cases (e.g., *Marbury v. Madison*), and evaluate real-world government decisions.
Transfer Learning	Applies knowledge to new situations, requiring critical thinking, problem-solving, and creativity.	Comparing Government Systems – Students contrast U.S. governance with parliamentary or authoritarian systems and propose constitutional amendments to address modern challenges.

As such, we have to figure out the right placement of small, doable habits and ensure consistency and precision through an easy-to-use visual guide.

Habit Placement

Every day in the classroom, we navigate the shifting terrain of student learning. Some students are racing ahead, others are making steady progress, and some seem stuck, struggling to grasp what we're teaching. This vast range of learning variability is precisely what makes teaching far more complex than tutoring—and why true learning rarely happens in a single leap. If it did, our profession wouldn't be called teaching, it would be called telling.

Dispositional Strategies Are Universal

There is a set of practices that matter everywhere—whether students are excelling or struggling. One immediate example that comes to mind is teacher–student relationships. Regardless of a student's proficiency, the relationships forged with students have a lasting impact on student learning regardless of the student's level of proficiency.

Often, these strategies are correlated to the learning of academic knowledge and skills, but they are more often directly connected to building the skills to become a better learner and person over time. These are the strategies that build student agency, metacognition, clarity, feedback literacy, social navigation, and self-regulation. In our work, we call this the dispositional zone, the core of learning where students develop the habits that allow them to learn how to learn.

Guy Claxton (2019) argues that these habits don't develop overnight. In fact, these habits require deliberate, sustained effort over the course of a K–12 education regardless of the zone. That's why, at the center of the Progress and Proficiency Framework, you'll find the zone dedicated to dispositional habits, the foundational skills that empower all learners.

Surface, Deep, and Transfer Strategies Are Situational

Once we understand where students are placed, then we need to identify where specific rigorous routines are placed within the framework or, more colloquially, map. John Hattie and Gregory Donoghue (2016) have shown that not all instructional strategies are universally effective—many are highly selective, working best in specific learning zones. A strategy that propels one group forward may have little impact with another in a different zone. This is typically associated with the strategies related to learning core content across surface, deep, and transfer levels. For instance, classroom discussion is highly effective at deep learning but does not carry the same yield at surface and transfer learning.

The need to scan such diversity of learning and adjust our teaching requires us to have a clear map of the terrain. We need a clear map of where our students are and how they are progressing. Then we must be able to adjust and choose the right strategy to move learners forward.

Habit Mapping

That's where the Progress and Proficiency Framework (see Figure 1) comes in. Imagine a grid where:
- The Y-axis represents proficiency—not as a fixed destination but across different types of learning (surface, deep, and transfer).
- The X-axis represents progress—the rate at which students are moving forward, whether measured through effect size (Cohen's D), RIT scores (NWEA), or classroom, school, or district proficiency levels.

Figure 1: Habit Mapping Matrix

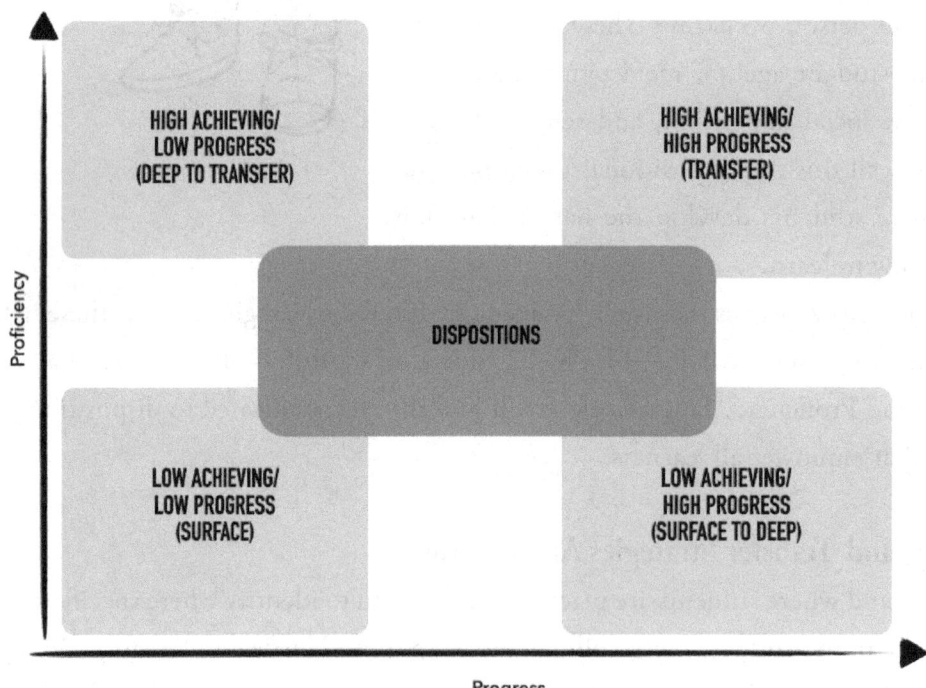

When we map student learning along these two dimensions, we see four distinct zones emerge:
1. High proficiency, high progress – Students excelling and accelerating.
2. High proficiency, low progress – Strong performers who may be coasting.
3. Low proficiency, high progress – Students making great strides but not yet proficient.
4. Low proficiency, low progress – Students struggling to move forward.

Where Do Strategies Belong?

In this book, along with Book 1 and Book 3, dispositional and competency-based routines have been categorized to help the reader determine which routines they should use to improve student learning. Before flipping to page____, look at the instructional practices outlined below. Where do you think they land in the Progress and Proficiency Framework?

Table 2: List of Strategies in Book 2

• 2 Box Induction	• In2Out Protocol
• 3 C's	• Jigsaw
• 4 A's Protocol	• Know/Need to Know List
• Assessment Scramble	• Matrix Problems
• Clues Approach	• Numberless/Slow Reveal
• Comparing Work Samples	• Red Team
• Compass Points	• Search and Unseen Questions
• Friendly Controversy	• Situation Room
• Frayer Model	• SPAR
• Gallery Walk	• To and Through
• Guided Practice	• Venn Diagram
• I Describe, You Draw	• Zoom In, Zoom Out

Which strategies are best suited for students making rapid progress at the surface, deep, and transfer levels?
- Which ones help students who are stagnant?
- Which ones seem universal, supporting students no matter where they are?
- Once you've made your predictions, turn the page and check your thinking. What did you get right? Where were you close? Where were you off? And, more importantly, why?

Once you have thought through these questions, take a look at Figure 2 on page 10.

Moving From Framework to Action

Now that we understand the framework, the real question is: How do we use it?
- In the classroom: How can we intentionally align strategies to students' zones?
- In a professional learning community (PLC): How can teams use this to diagnose learning needs and plan instruction?
- As a school: How does this shape professional development and intervention structures?
- As a coach: How can we help teachers apply this thinking in real time?

To answer these questions, let's think about our proactive and reactive moves.

Proactive: What do we do before students walk into the room? This is our first-best instruction—our plan for success before we even see results from our first formative assessment move.

Reactive: What do we do once we have evidence? How do we adjust when students don't respond as expected? Or are we, in fact, ahead of our initial plan?

So, as we dive deeper into strategies, keep these two approaches in mind. Where do your standards require you to start proactively, and where do students fall on the map as you progress? How will you navigate this terrain to get to your destination with students?

Let's look at some small, doable routines that can get us there.

Figure 2: Habit Mapping Example

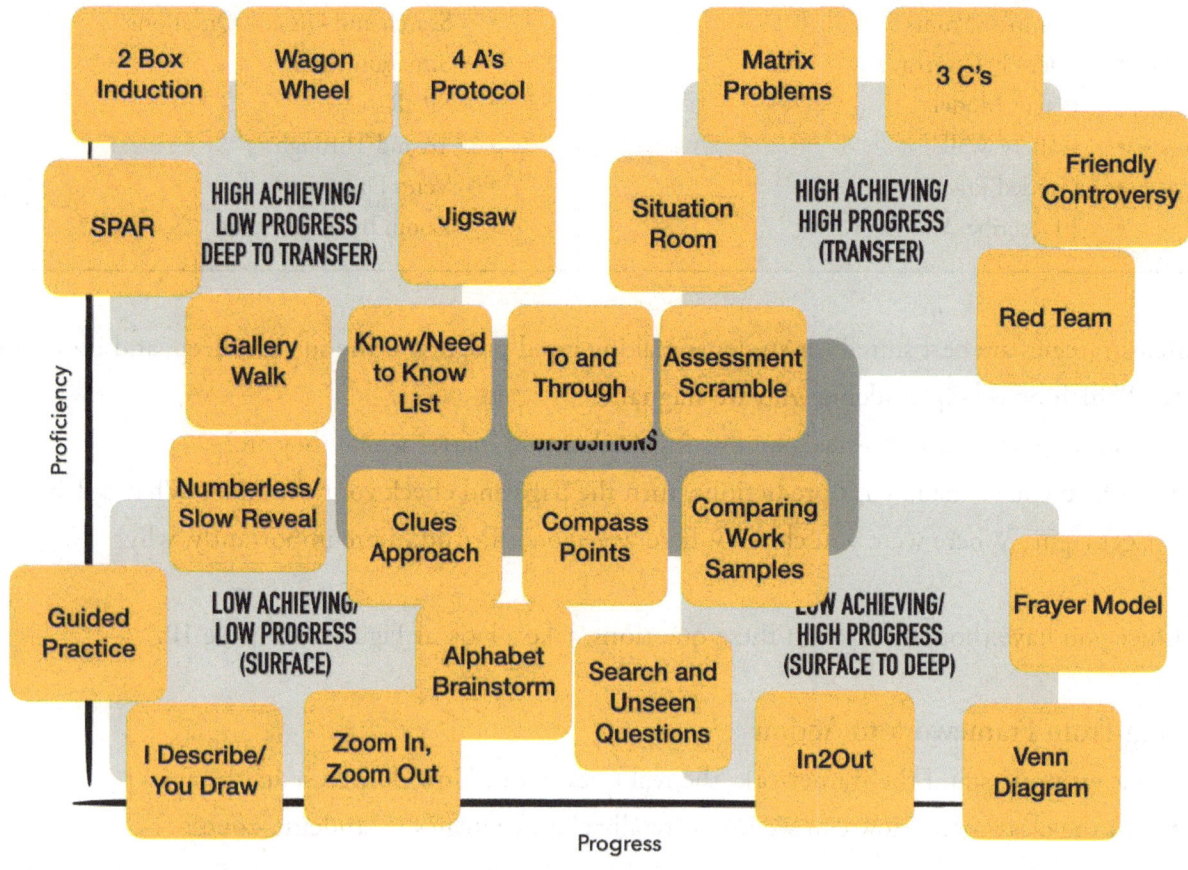

Habit Placement & Sequence in Rigorous PBL by Design

Rigorous project-based learning (RPBL) stands as a formidable tool in shaping students' dispositional habits and fostering holistic learning across surface, deep, and transfer learning levels. At its core, PBL isn't solely about cultivating critical skills and mindsets necessary for success beyond the classroom; it's also about imparting and building knowledge. By integrating rigorous PBL into teaching and learning, educators can strategically develop students' abilities to transfer knowledge, delve into deeper understanding, and master foundational concepts while engaging students in interesting problems and building their agency.

The methodology of rigorous PBL follows a well-defined sequence that commences and culminates with transfer learning, while ensuring comprehensive engagement with surface and deep learning through a unit of study. During the project, students should be moving between each phase of learning as new learning is uncovered and students are working through solutions to transfer. In essence, the methodology is book-ended by transfer learning (see Figure 3).

Phase 1, the Project Launch, serves as the foundation, setting the context and objectives for the ensuing journey across surface, deep, and transfer learning. During this phase, students are introduced to real-world problems or challenges, building their curiosity, prompting them to contemplate potential solutions, and asking questions related to the building blocks of content and skills they will need to solve the problem effectively. This initial phase primes students for the complexities they'll encounter, establishing the overarching purpose of their learning journey.

Phase 2, the Surface Workshops, focuses on equipping students with the fundamental knowledge and skills necessary to navigate the project successfully. Through targeted workshops, students engage in activities that address surface-level understanding of relevant concepts and methodologies. This phase serves as a scaffold, providing students with the necessary groundwork to tackle the project's challenges effectively. By solidifying their grasp of foundational concepts, students lay the groundwork for deeper exploration and analysis.

Phase 3, the Deep Workshops, delves into the intricacies of the subject matter, encouraging students to explore concepts with depth and nuance. Here, students engage in activities designed to relate core concepts to establish an understanding of principles, theories, and tested and untested ideas within a discipline. Moreover, this phase fosters students' critical thinking, problem-solving, and analytical skills. Through discussions, evaluation, and reflection, and seeking help from peers, students develop a profound understanding of the underlying principles driving the project. This phase encourages students to think beyond the surface, probing deeper into the complexities of the subject matter and uncovering connections that might otherwise remain obscured.

Phase 4, the Project Conclusion/Reflection, represents the culmination of the PBL journey, where students showcase their learning and insights gleaned throughout the process. Students build their transfer-level habits and present their projects to peers, educators, and potentially even real-world stakeholders. Here, students are challenged to articulate their findings, defend their conclusions, and reflect on their learning journey. This final phase not only reinforces transfer learning by applying newfound knowledge in a practical context but also encourages metacognition as students reflect on their growth, challenges overcome, and areas for future improvement. In essence, rigorous PBL not only fosters surface, deep, and transfer learning but also cultivates the dispositional habits essential for lifelong learning and success.

Figure 3: Re-Envisioning Rigorous PBL

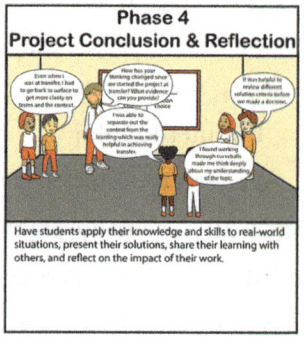

This book serves as a comprehensive guide to implementing RPBL effectively, offering step-by-step visuals that streamline the process across all four phases. Each phase is meticulously broken down into four steps, providing educators with clear and concise visual guides on how to navigate through the complexities of the methodology. Through simple and straightforward pictures with steps, educators are equipped with the tools they need to facilitate a seamless PBL experience for their students.

Table 3: Instructional routines at each project stage

Phase 1 Project Launch	Phase 2 Surface Workshops	Phase 3 Deep Workshops	Phase 4 Project Conclusion and Reflection
Instructional Routines	Instructional Routines	Instructional Routines	Instructional Routines
• Matrix Problems • Clues Approach • Assessment Scramble • Know/Need to Know List • To and Through • Compass Points	• Zoom In, Zoom Out • Search and Unseen Questions • Comparing Work Samples • Guided Practice • Numberless/ Slow Reveal • I Describe, You Draw • Alphabet Brainstorm	• Venn Diagram • 2 Box Induction • 4 A's Protocol • SPAR • Frayer Model • In2Out Protocol	• 3 C's • Jigsaw • Red Team • Situation Room • Friendly Controversy • Gallery Walk • Wagon Wheel

Four-Square Routines Within the Rigorous PBL Methodology

This book is part of a three-book series that provides rigorous routines that support teachers in ensuring students develop the dispositions and competencies necessary for learning at high levels across a range of complex tasks and situations. The following table illustrates how each routine in the other two books are aligned to Rigorous PBL by Design.

Table 4: Alignment of instruction routines from Re-Envisioning Rigor books 1 and 3 in PBL.

	Phase 1 Project Launch	Phase 2 Surface Workshops	Phase 3 Deep Workshops	Phase 4 Project Conclusion and Reflection
		Instructional Routines		
Book 1	• Learning GPS • Zones of Learning • Silent Protocol • Work Sample Protocol • What? So What? Now What? • I Used to Think . . . Now I Think . . .	• Direct Modeling • Backward Fading • Harkness Protocol • Choral and Echo Reading • Mnemonics • Summarize the Story So Far	• Turn and Talk With Conjunctions • Dots Protocol • Final Word Protocol • Picture Worth 1,000 Words • Text to Text, Text to Self, Text to World • Socratic Seminar	• Analogies and Metaphors • Curveballs and Sequels • Generating Hypotheses • Town Hall Meeting • World Café • Chalk Talk
Book 3	• Green and Red • Consultancy Dilemma • KWL Chart • Self- and Small Group Quizzing • Error Analysis • Known, Nuance, and Novel • Shadow Protocol • Talk Detectives	• TAG protocol • Four Corners • What Makes You Say That? • Spot It, Fix It (:30 to 5) • Tea Party • Odd One Out • S-I-T Protocol • Opinion Lines	• Sticky Note Protocol • Question Before Comments • Perspective Analysis • Elaborative Interrogation • Tuning Protocol • Rapid Writing • Semantic Webbing • Reciprocal Teaching	• 5 Whys • Realm of Concern • Empathy Protocols • Examining Errors • Hot Seat • Fishbone • Headlines • Three Stories

Breaking Rigorous Routines Into Visual Steps

This book is designed to cut through the conceptual verbiage that requires teachers to imagine what strategies may look like and feel like and offers step-by-step pictures to illustrate complex moves in a concrete and precise manner. This, we think, will help readers identify the nuance clearly and aid in precision of practice. Akin to a playbook laying out visual steps for a play on the field, this book provides four easy-to-understand steps for implementing and assessing impact on the routine use and outcome of a number of teaching strategies. Of course, this book narrows those strategies down to those practices that are necessary for today's learners and most critical for impact

Figure 5: *The Five Guiding Principles*

1. **Progressing Toward Rigorous Teaching and Learning**
   - Rigor isn't about flashy initiatives; it's built through small, consistent, high-impact actions.
   - The focus is on developing students' dispositional and competency-based habits (surface, deep, and transfer learning) to build agency and tackle complex challenges.

2. **Developing Clarity and Ensuring Accessibility**
   - Visuals provide clarity, making strategies easy to understand and apply.
   - Strategies are adaptable across diverse classroom contexts and subject areas.
   - Designed to meet the needs of all learners, including neurodiverse students and those from varied backgrounds.

3. **Anchoring Toward Concrete Examples**
   - Learning is more effective when teachers see practical, real-world applications.
   - Visual guides offer tangible examples to scaffold understanding and implementation.

4. **Consistency and Precision**
   - Small, sustainable habits drive lasting instructional improvement.
   - The 1% better approach ensures steady progress without overwhelming teachers.
   - Visual references promote consistency and precision in instructional practices.

5. **Scaffolded Support**
   - Provides "just right" guidance through visual references and inquiry-based learning.
   - Ensures instructional consistency across classrooms and subjects.
   - Acts as a powerful playbook for PLCs, supporting collective efficacy.
   - Serves as a scaffold for new teachers, breaking down strategies into manageable steps.
   - Supports professional development by offering a shared language and ongoing reinforcement.

How to Use the Visual Guide

This visual guide is not designed for passive study. Instead, think of it as a field guide for teachers to enhance their practice. The visual guide offers a range of strategies that serve to develop students' dispositions of learning and core competency across surface, deep, and transfer learning. Over time, you will gain a comprehensive understanding of these strategies and learn to apply them in your classroom with confidence, creating an environment that fosters effective teaching and meaningful learning.

Each strategy spans two pages: the left page includes a description and dashboard, while the right features a four-square graphic detailing implementation steps.

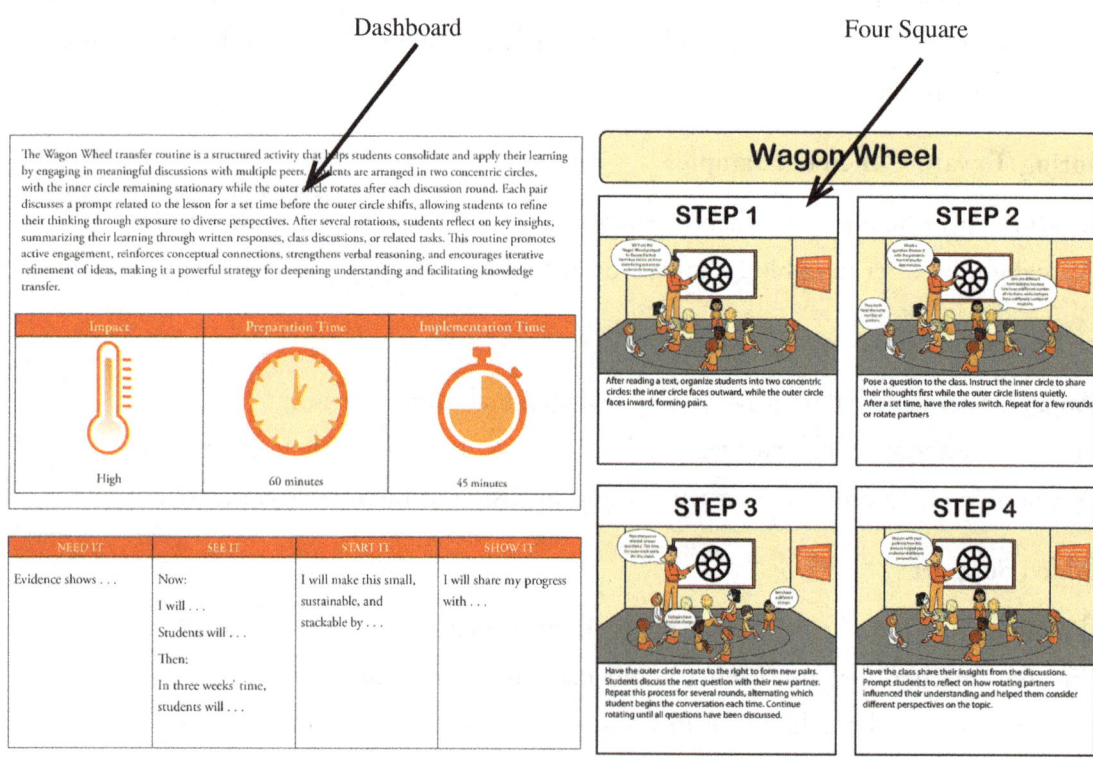

Figure 6: Dashboard and Four Square

Dashboard & Icons (Left-Hand Page)

The dashboard provides key guidance for implementing each strategy, helping teachers make informed, efficient decisions.

How to Use It

- Description – Brief overview of the strategy, its purpose, and ideal placement in a lesson.
- Dashboard – Quick-reference guide for impact, prep time, and implementation time.

Icons & Their Meaning

1. **Impact** – Shows the strategy's effect size, based on research-backed studies.
2. **Preparation Time** – Estimated setup time in 15-minute intervals (never exceeding an hour).
3. **Implementation Time** – Time needed to use the strategy with students, decreasing with practice.

By considering impact and time requirements, teachers can strategically integrate these practices into their curriculum for maximum effectiveness.

The First Icon: Impact

Figure 7: Re-Envisioning Rigor Icons

The Four-Square Steps (Right-Hand Page)

The four-square design simplifies complexity by breaking instruction into four clear steps, bridging theory and practice. This approach helps educators plan, implement, and assess instruction effectively while keeping the focus on meaningful student learning.

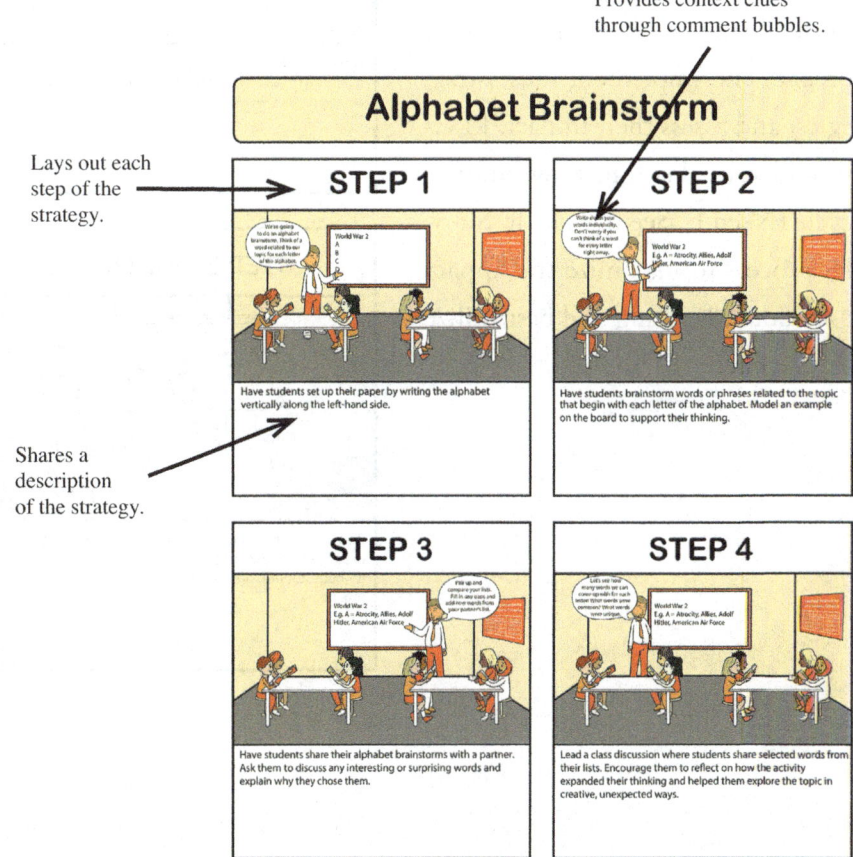

RE-ENVISIONING RIGOR

How to Use the Guide:

1. Read Each Step's Description: Review the caption under each graphic for key concepts and strategies.
2. Examine the Visuals: Analyze student positioning, classroom setup, and available resources to see the strategy in action.
3. Explore the Speech Bubbles: Gain insights from real educators through comments and explanations embedded in the visuals.
4. Connect Theory to Practice: Adapt strategies to your classroom by integrating descriptions, visuals, and insights into your teaching.

Using the Guide for Collaborative Professional Learning

High-functioning PLCs are adept at identifying specific areas of student needs. Team members can use this book to identify strategies that can most effectively meet these needs, prepare and implement those strategies, and assess their impact. PLCs should use the following inquiry cycle (Need It, See It, Start It, Show It) process to maximize the impact on student learning and best utilize this resource.

Figure 9: The Need It, See It, Start It, Show It Framework

NEED IT	SEE IT	START IT	SHOW IT
Evidence shows . . .	Now: I will . . . Students will . . . Then: In three weeks' time, students will . . .	I will make this small, sustainable, and stackable by . . .	I will share my progress with . . .

Figure 10: The Need It, See It, Start It, Show It Framework

Use this framework to effectively understand, implement, and assess instructional strategies. A space is provided for you and your team to take notes.

1. **Need It: Identify the Purpose**
   - Determine why this strategy is necessary.
   - Use evidence such as student work, assessment data, or stakeholder feedback to justify implementation.
   - Reference tools for gathering evidence to support your decision.

2. **See It: Make It Observable**
   - Focus on how the four steps of the strategy should appear in practice.
   - Identify what changes in both teacher and student behaviors will indicate implementation.
   - Consider the immediate impact and how it should evolve over time.

3. **Start It: Lower the Implementation Barrier**
   - Ensure the strategy is easy to integrate into existing routines.
   - Use habit-stacking techniques to embed it into daily practice.
   - Shrink the change by making implementation manageable and sustainable.

4. **Show It: Share Progress and Evidence**
   - Track and present evidence of implementation over time.
   - Engage in collaborative reflection—what's working, what's not, and why.
   - Frame successes and challenges constructively to improve individual and collective practice.

Visit Mimi & Todd Press for a glossary, videos, and other resources that will support your learning with A Visual, Step-By-Step Guide For Re-Envisioning Rigor: Powerful Routines For Promoting Learning At High Levels.

https://qrco.de/Re-Rigor2

Phase 1: Project Launch

The Project Launch is the first phase of the rigorous project-based learning (PBL) process. This stage introduces students to complex, real-world problems that require sustained inquiry and problem-solving over the coming days, weeks, or months. Students engage in exploratory activities that immerse them in the problem context, clarify project expectations, assess their current knowledge and skills, and establish a plan of action individually and/or with teams.

To ensure clarity and direction, this phase includes structured protocols, such as Matrix Problems, the Clues Approach, and Assessment Scramble, which help students engage with the problem at a transfer level from the start. Once the project is launched, additional protocols, including the Know/Need to Know List, To and Through, and Compass Points, guide students in setting learning goals and identifying next steps. This foundational phase builds students' assessment capabilities as well as prepares them for the phases of the project that require problem-solving and developing competency across surface, deep, and transfer learning levels.

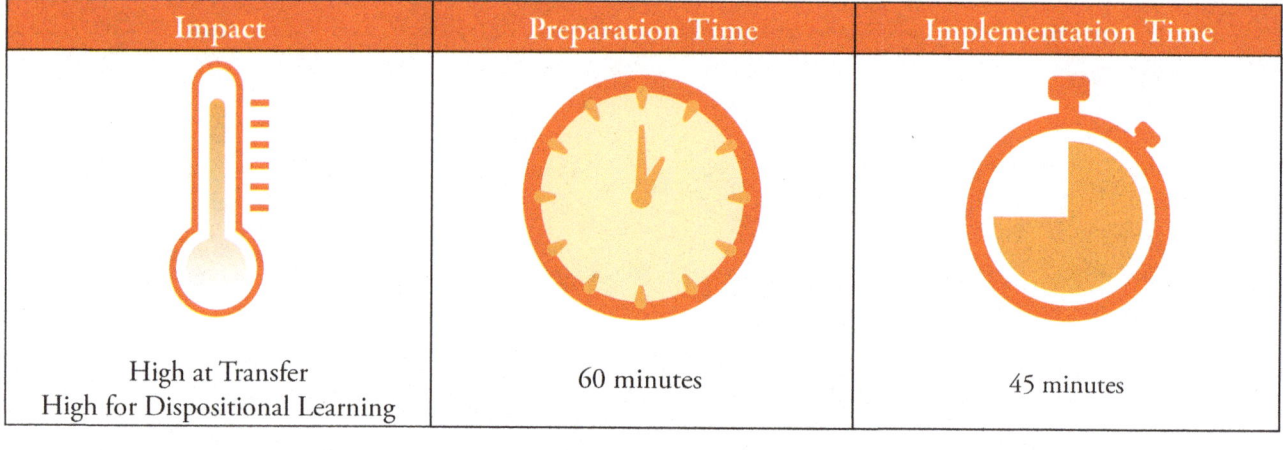

Impact	Preparation Time	Implementation Time
High at Transfer High for Dispositional Learning	60 minutes	45 minutes

NEED IT	SEE IT	START IT	SHOW IT
Evidence shows . . .	Now: I will . . . Students will . . . Then: In three weeks' time, students will . . .	I will make this small, sustainable, and stackable by . . .	I will share my progress with . . .

PHASE ONE — PROJECT LAUNCH

PHASE 1: PROJECT LAUNCH

STEP 1

Present a transfer-level problem to students by inviting a community member to share a real-world challenge. Using student obervations from campus to spark inquiry, or arranging a presentation from an outside expert that connects classroom learning to complex, authentic contexts.

STEP 2

Have students work in pairs to identify or develop a driving question. Then, ask them to create a list of "need to knows" that will help them explore and answer the question.

STEP 3

Give each student group a set of success criteria written on individual strips of paper. Ask them to sort the criteria into three categories based on complexity: surface, deep and transfer. Then, have groups compare and discuss how their sorting decisions differ or align with those of the other groups.

STEP 4

Ask students to write and post the next steps they will take to meet the success criteria. Then have them explain how these steps will help them answer the driving question.

Matrix Problems

The Matrix Problems protocol encourages students to make connections across diverse scenarios, developing analytical skills by drawing parallels between different contexts. Through collaborative discussion, students not only deepen their understanding of core concepts but also enhance critical thinking by formulating questions that bridge various real-world situations. This method builds a foundation for complex problem-solving and helps students develop a more integrated approach to learning. By actively engaging in this process, students refine their ability to apply knowledge across contexts, preparing them for more advanced, interdisciplinary challenges.

Impact	Preparation Time	Implementation Time
High	45 minutes	6–20 minutes

NEED IT	SEE IT	START IT	SHOW IT
Evidence shows . . .	Now: I will . . . Students will . . . Then: In three weeks' time, students will . . .	I will make this small, sustainable, and stackable by . . .	I will share my progress with . . .

PHASE ONE — PROJECT LAUNCH

Matrix Problems

STEP 1

Share with students that you will present multiple context or ideas and ask them to write down what they know about each one. Explain that they will work together to identify the connections between the situations. These connections will form the learning intention and success criteria for the unit.
Use a Venn Diagram to organize their thoughts.

STEP 2

Show students additional information about each context or idea that relate to a specific learning intention and success criteria. This could be done in multiple ways including showing videos, written work samples, audio recordings, or news articles. Ask students to fill in the Venn Diagram with further details.

STEP 3

Ask students to brainstorm the learning intention and success criteria and place the answers into the middle bubble.
Show students the actual answers and ask them to identify their successes and challenges in identifying the goals for learning.

STEP 4

Prompt students to generate a new context that connect to the learning intention and success criteria.

Clues Approach

The Clues Approach protocol fosters a collaborative learning environment where students actively participate in clarifying expectations and providing teachers with essential assessment data. Initially, teachers introduce the unit by explaining objectives and connecting the content to real-world applications, engaging students in brainstorming sessions to gather initial thoughts and prior knowledge. Through interactive discussions, students and teachers co-construct learning intentions/goals and success criteria, visually representing these expectations for ongoing reference. Formative assessments are designed based on the gathered clues, with regular check-ins to monitor progress and adjust instruction. Differentiated instruction is implemented to address diverse learning needs, offering targeted support and enrichment activities. Reflection and feedback are integral, encouraging student self-assessment and providing specific teacher feedback.

Impact	Preparation Time	Implementation Time
High	5 minutes	15–30 minutes

NEED IT	SEE IT	START IT	SHOW IT
Evidence shows . . .	Now: I will . . . Students will . . . Then: In three weeks' time, students will . . .	I will make this small, sustainable, and stackable by . . .	I will share my progress with . . .

PHASE ONE — PROJECT LAUNCH

Clues Approach

STEP 1

Provide students with the learning intention and verbs associated with the success criteria. Next give students an example of work ("a clue") and ask them to create the success criteria.

STEP 2

Place students into pairs and have them create a set of criteria. After a few minutes, have students meet in larger groups of 4-6 to share their criteria and develop an agreed upon list.

STEP 3

Provide students with the actual rubric and have them compare their own rubric with the teacher's constructed rubric. During this comparison students should identify their range of accuracy (e.g. We are close...We are correct...We were missing...).

STEP 4

Ask students to do the following:
1. List the main criteria that were different from what they expected to learn.
2. Share these criteria with classmates to find similarities and differences.
3. Write down these differences to review at the start of each class.

Assessment Scramble

The Assessment Scramble strategy involves giving students a set of questions or tasks in a scrambled or randomized order, promoting deeper understanding by requiring them to apply their knowledge in varied contexts. Used as a preassessment, this approach helps to identify students' initial knowledge and misconceptions. It connects seamlessly with the Know/Need to Know process, where students identify what they already understand and what they need to learn. By navigating through randomized tasks, students engage in critical thinking and problem-solving, reinforcing their learning and adaptability. This method provides teachers with valuable insights into student understanding and readiness, allowing for more tailored and effective instruction throughout the unit.

Impact	Preparation Time	Implementation Time
High	45 minutes	6–20 minutes

NEED IT	SEE IT	START IT	SHOW IT
Evidence shows . . .	Now: I will . . . Students will . . . Then: In three weeks' time, students will . . .	I will make this small, sustainable, and stackable by . . .	I will share my progress with . . .

PHASE ONE — PROJECT LAUNCH

Assessment Scramble

STEP 1

Place individual questions from a test on individual sheets of paper. The questions should be across levels of complexity and related to the same learning intentions and success criteria.

STEP 2

Ask students to sort the questions into levels of complexity. Provide sample verbs that serve as a clue for organization. Walk around the room and monitor their progress. When students are incorrect in their sorting, provide them with corrective feedback.

STEP 3

Ask students to brainstorm possible learning intentions and success criteria. Provide a gentle reminder to separate context from content (e.g. Separate out what you will be learning from what you will be learning it through).

STEP 4

Give students that actual learning intention and success criteria. Ask them to compare their ideas from yours. Consider using known, nuance, novel or used to think . . . Now I think to make this comparison. If time permits, ask them to generate other transfer problems that could be solved.

Know/Need to Know List

The following routine helps students categorize their current understanding with aspirational knowledge through questioning.

Know (K): Refers to the existing knowledge and skills that students bring to the project.

This includes prior knowledge of the subject matter, relevant skills, and any background information that may be helpful.

Need to Know (NTK): Refers to the new knowledge and skills that students need to acquire in order to complete the project successfully. This includes key concepts, essential skills, and specific information relevant to the project's goals and objectives. Identifying the "need to know" helps teachers focus instruction on the most critical learning objectives. This is usually presented as a T-Chart in the classroom for students to reference each day. In addition, the K/NTK list should adapt as the class progresses with new learning. Teachers should monitor the students' questions to see if they are getting more specific and complex.

Impact	Preparation Time	Implementation Time
High for Dispositional Learning	Less than 15 minutes	1–5 minutes

NEED IT	SEE IT	START IT	SHOW IT
Evidence shows . . .	Now: I will . . . Students will . . . Then: In three weeks' time, students will . . .	I will make this small, sustainable, and stackable by . . .	I will share my progress with . . .

PHASE ONE — PROJECT LAUNCH

Know and Need to Know List

STEP 1

Introduce the project context, learning intentions, and success criteria. Next, ask students to share what they already "know" about the project, learning intentions, and success criteria. During these discussions, it is important to ensure students have access to entry events, rubrics, pre-assessment data, and/or work samples to reference.

STEP 2

Ask students to group their "knows" across surface, deep, and transfer. If needed, provide sample verbs to support their statement.

STEP 3

Ask students to group their Need to Know across surface, deep, and transfer. If needed, provide sample verbs to support their questioning.

STEP 4

Use the evolving list to identify next steps in learning. Review and modify the list over the course of the unit or project. Make sure to discuss with students how the questions are expanding into deep or transfer or moving to a greater level of surface questions.

To and Through

The To and Through strategy emphasizes the crucial distinction between the context and the actual substance (content) of what is being learned. This clarity-oriented practice enables students to make a distinction between the material they are learning and the broader context in which it exists. The phrase "To and Through" encapsulates the dual focus on both the path leading to knowledge versus the task students are completing or the context students are learning the knowledge through. The essence of To and Through lies in its dual focus:

To: Refers to the pathway leading students to the essential knowledge or skill. This involves the preliminary steps, background information, and preparatory activities that pave the way for understanding the core material.

Through: Refers to the process and context through which students engage with and internalize the core material. This involves the specific tasks, exercises, discussions, and applications that immerse students in the learning process.

Impact	Preparation Time	Implementation Time
High	5 minutes	3–6 minutes

NEED IT	SEE IT	START IT	SHOW IT
Evidence shows . . .	Now: I will . . . Students will . . . Then: In three weeks' time, students will . . .	I will make this small, sustainable, and stackable by . . .	I will share my progress with . . .

PHASE ONE — PROJECT LAUNCH

To and Through

STEP 1

Review the learning intentions and success criteria with students and ensure that all tasks and contexts have been removed. The learning intentions and success criteria should only show the exact expectations of the content.

STEP 2

Provide students with a number of examples of context and content and share that the context is what we are learning something through and the content is what we are learning to understand and do. For instance, we are learning to understand solids, liquids, and gasses through making slime.

STEP 3

Provide a number of examples and ask students to identify the content and the context and share their responses with a partner. If students are struggling, give additional examples and walk students through the reason one is context and another is content.

STEP 4

During lessons, stop the class and ask students to do what they are learning (e.g. "We are learning about repeated theme in a text through reading To Kill a Mockingbird).
Based on student responses, determine what actions are needed to strengthen their clarity.

Compass Points

The Compass Points routine is a reflective strategy that helps students analyze ideas, perspectives, or decisions from multiple angles, fostering critical thinking and deeper understanding. Using the four cardinal directions as a guide, students respond to specific prompts: E (Excited)—what excites or interests them about the topic; W (Worrisome)—what concerns or challenges they anticipate; N (Need to Know)—what additional information or questions they have; and S (Stance or Suggestion)—their overall perspective or proposed action. By systematically considering these different aspects, students develop a more balanced and thoughtful approach to complex topics. This routine encourages engagement, inquiry, and structured thinking, making it a valuable tool for discussions, decision-making, and content exploration.

Impact	Preparation Time	Implementation Time
High	45 minutes	6–20 minutes

NEED IT	SEE IT	START IT	SHOW IT
Evidence shows . . .	Now: I will . . . Students will . . . Then: In three weeks' time, students will . . .	I will make this small, sustainable, and stackable by . . .	I will share my progress with . . .

PHASE ONE — PROJECT LAUNCH

Compass Points

STEP 1

Speech/labels: E = Excites; "Let's reflect. What excites you about your current progress?"; "I need more deliberate practice, but I am getting better."; "I have all of the surface and deep, but still need transfer."; "I have begun to transfer, but still need to practice some surface learning."; "Exemplars helped me improve my work."

Have students work in pairs to reflect on their current progress in meeting learning goals. Each student answers a series of questions and shows evidence to back up their progress. Throughout each step, monitor pairs by walking around the room and listening in. Pause the class after each step and summarize what you are hearing. Start with the question: What excites you about your current progress?

STEP 2

Speech/labels: W = Worrisome; "What do you find worrisome about your current progress?"; "Not meeting all the transfer level learning expectations."; "I'm worried I will procrastinate."; "I'm worried that I don't understand all the factual information."; "I'm worried about the feedback I will receive."

Repeat this process with the following question: What do you find worrisome about your current progress?

STEP 3

Speech/labels: "What are your 'need to knows'?"; N = Need to Know; "I need to understand the various analogies we studied."; "I need to know how to remember all the information in my notes."

Repeat this process with the following question: What do you need to know to be successful?

STEP 4

Speech/labels: "What suggestions do you have to improve your learning?"; S = Stance or Suggestion Moving Forward; "I need to practice by reviewing previous analogies shown in class."; "I need to create flash cards and then practice."

Repeat this process with the following question: What suggestions do you have to improve your learning?

Phase 2: Surface Workshop

In the second phase of rigorous project-based learning (PBL), explicit instructional practices ensure students develop the foundational knowledge and skills necessary for deeper inquiry. This phase emphasizes direct modeling, where teachers break down complex concepts, introduce essential vocabulary, and guide students through key ideas using structured, intentional instruction. Strategies such as Zoom In, Zoom Out help students focus on critical details before stepping back to see the broader context, while Search and Unseen Questions and Comparing Work Samples differentiate inquiry, ensuring all students engage with content meaningfully. Checking for understanding throughout this process allows teachers to provide real-time feedback and adjust instruction based on student needs.

As students build their conceptual foundation, they transition into guided practice, where they actively participate in structured learning experiences alongside teachers. Protocols such as Numberless/Slow Reveal help students develop problem-solving strategies without relying on immediate answers, while I Describe, You Draw reinforces precision in communication and conceptual understanding. This blend of direct modeling and guided practice ensures that students are not passive recipients of information but are actively engaged in constructing knowledge. By focusing on clarity, scaffolding, and intentional checks for understanding, this phase equips students with the skills and confidence needed to navigate deeper analysis and complex problem-solving in later stages of PBL.

Impact	Preparation Time	Implementation Time
High	45 minutes	6–20 minutes

NEED IT	SEE IT	START IT	SHOW IT
Evidence shows . . .	Now: I will . . . Students will . . . Then: In three weeks' time, students will . . .	I will make this small, sustainable, and stackable by . . .	I will share my progress with . . .

PHASE 2: SURFACE WORKSHOP

Surface Workshop

STEP 1

Return to the "Need to Know" list created during the project launch. Remind students that this list outlines the key content, concepts, and skills they will need to successfully answer the driving question. Choose one essential item from the list, something students cannot move forward without, and model it explicity. Use clear examples, think aloud strategies, and visual tools to show not just how to do it, but why it matters for the work ahead.

STEP 2

Ask purposeful questions and after modeling to uncover how well students understand the concept or skill. Use a mix of surface-level questions (e.g., definitions, recall, identification) and deeper prompts (e.g., explain, justify) to get a fuller picture of student thinking. Pay close attention to misconceptions, partial understandings, or areas of confusion. Based on what you hear, adapt your instruction. This might mean rephrasing an idea or modeling again in a differnt way.

STEP 3

Support students with targeted reading, writing, and discussion tasks that help them build essential knowledge and fluency related to the content. These surface-level tasks should reinforce key terms and ideas. As students work, circulate to listen, prompt, and question. Use real-time feedback to help students clarify their thinking, correct misunderstandings, and build confidence in applying what they've learned.

STEP 4

Review student responses, work, and reflections to determine whether they are ready for independent practice or still need support. Look for patterns in understanding and areas of confusion. If students are not yet confident or accurate, go back to earlier steps such as modeling the concept again or offering more guided practice. The goal is to make sure students are prepared to apply their learning with success.

Zoom In, Zoom Out

The Zoom In, Zoom Out process can be used to shift focus between specific details and broader contexts, aiming to deepen understanding by shifting perspectives and scales of analysis. The teacher "zooms in" by focusing on specific details, examples, or data points to provide a deep understanding of a particular concept or phenomenon. This might involve analyzing a text passage, dissecting a scientific experiment, or examining a historical event in detail.

The teacher then "zooms out" by stepping back to broaden the perspective, connecting the specific details back to larger themes, contexts, or historical trends. This helps students see the bigger picture and understand how the specific concept or event fits into a larger framework.

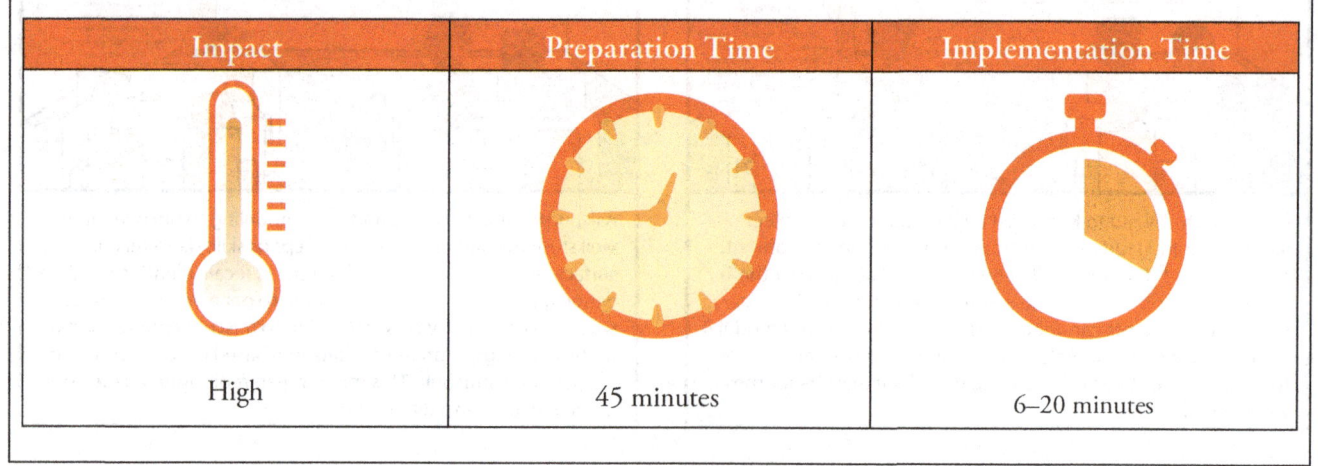

Impact	Preparation Time	Implementation Time
High	45 minutes	6–20 minutes

NEED IT	SEE IT	START IT	SHOW IT
Evidence shows . . .	Now: I will . . . Students will . . . Then: In three weeks' time, students will . . .	I will make this small, sustainable, and stackable by . . .	I will share my progress with . . .

PHASE 2: SURFACE WORKSHOP

Zoom In, Zoom Out

STEP 1

Today we are going to "Zoom out" to the cell and "Zoom in" to the parts of the cell called organelles.

Introduce a broad overview of a concepts (e.g. Cell Structure and Function) using a visual (e.g timeline or concept map).

STEP 2

Let's zoom in. Here is an organelle called a ribosome. This organelle . . .

Introduce a specific aspect of the concept (e.g., endoplasmic reticulum), and both model and discuss the explicit link between the broader concept and the specific aspect under study.

STEP 3

Now that we have looked at three different organelles, let's zoom back out to see how this connects to the cell. What connections do you see?

The different organelles all work like tiny organs to make sure the cell functions.

Continue this process by showing the link between the broader concept and the specific aspect under study. Have students work in pairs to discuss and then share the explicit connections.

STEP 4

Let's find more connections between cell parts and see how they help the cell function in it's surroundings.

This time let's respond by using an analogy or metaphor to relate the parts of the cell.

The cell works like an assembly line. The assembly line workers (ribosomes) read blueprints (mRNA) to know what type of car (protein) to assemble. The blueprints come from the design office (nucleus).

Repeat Steps 1-3. Each time you repeat the process, expect students to increase the complexity of their answers. In pairs have them share their responses in class.

Adapted from the work of Sherrington and Goodwin 2022.

Search and Unseen Questions

This strategy is designed to help students distinguish between what is explicitly stated and what requires deeper inquiry. Students first identify "Seen" questions, which can be answered directly using available information, such as facts from a text, image, or lesson. They then generate "Unseen" questions, which go beyond the given information, requiring inference, interpretation, or further research. This routine encourages curiosity and helps students recognize gaps in their understanding, laying the foundation for deeper exploration. By categorizing questions in this way, students develop a habit of critically analyzing information while building inquiry skills that support both comprehension and future learning.

Impact	Preparation Time	Implementation Time
High	45 minutes	6–20 minutes

NEED IT	SEE IT	START IT	SHOW IT
Evidence shows . . .	Now: I will . . . Students will . . . Then: In three weeks' time, students will . . .	I will make this small, sustainable, and stackable by . . .	I will share my progress with . . .

PHASE 2: SURFACE WORKSHOP

Search and Unseen Questions

STEP 1

Let's start by noticing what the text says directly. What details or facts stand out to you?

I see that the author mentions the main character's struggle with moving to a new city. That seems important.

Begin by prompting students with search questions that guide them to locate specific information in the text, image, or film. These questions focus on concrete details that are directly observable or stated. This phase builds surface-level understanding and ensures students can comprehend explicit content before moving to deeper analysis.

STEP 2

How does this part connect to what we read earlier or to something you already know?

The struggle with moving reminds me of the character's backstory from earlier. It explains why they're feeling out of place.

Encourage students to make connections between ideas and clarify initial understanding, linking explicit details to prior knowledge or previous parts of the text.

STEP 3

What do you think the author is suggesting here, even if it's not stated directly?

I think the character's isolation is more than just the move. Maybe they're struggling with their identity too.

Shift to deeper questioning by prompting students to infer meaning beyond what's explicitly stated. To do this, ask unseen questions that prompt students to read between the lines, such as: Why do you think the character acted that way? What is the author suggesting here? How does this idea relate to something we have seen before?

STEP 4

How could this idea connect to real-life experiences or what might it mean beyond the text?

This reminds me of times I felt out of place. It makes me think the author is exploring how we all search for belonging in different ways.

Conclude by asking students to reflect on their insights and extend their thinking, considering how these ideas apply to broader themes or other contexts.

Adapted from the work of Sherrington and Goodwin 2022.

Comparing Work Samples

Teachers provide students with examples of high-quality work that demonstrate the desired learning outcomes. Students compare their own work to the model, identifying strengths and areas for improvement. Students use exemplars, rubrics, and checklists to provide clear criteria for success, allowing students to compare their work to the expected standards and adjust their approach accordingly. Students compare and discuss each other's work in pairs or small groups, using teacher-provided prompts or questions to identify strengths and offer constructive feedback.

Impact	Preparation Time	Implementation Time
High	5 minutes	20–25 minutes

NEED IT	SEE IT	START IT	SHOW IT
Evidence shows . . .	Now: I will . . . Students will . . . Then: In three weeks' time, students will . . .	I will make this small, sustainable, and stackable by . . .	I will share my progress with . . .

PHASE 2: SURFACE WORKSHOP

Comparing Work Samples

STEP 1

Present students with a strong work sample that nearly meets the success criteria. Ask students to review the piece, evaluate it using the learning intention and success criteria, and assign it a score. Facilitate a discussion about what makes it effective and where it could be improved.

STEP 2

Share a work sample with students that is sub-par. Ask them to rank the piece based on the learning intention and success criteria. Have them compare this piece with the near perfect example.

STEP 3

Ask students to suggest specific strategies that could improve Work Sample 2. While students share, listen for references to the learning intention, success criteria, and other work samples. If students are not using the success criteria to justify their suggestions, redirect them to do so.

STEP 4

In pairs, ask students to repeat the process with a partner. Have each student go through steps 1-3 with their partner's piece of work. After this process, give students 3 minutes to make an immediate change to their own work and then share that change to their partner.

Guided Practice

Guided Practice is a strategy where the teacher actively guides students through a new skill or concept, providing essential support and scaffolding to facilitate practice and mastery. Often considered the "middle step" between direct instruction (where the teacher explicitly explains the concept) and independent practice (where students apply the skill on their own), guided practice bridges the gap between theory and application. During this phase, the teacher works closely with students, offering immediate feedback, clarifying misunderstandings, and modeling the thought processes required for the task. This collaborative approach allows students to gradually build confidence and competence, ensuring they have a solid grasp of the concept before moving on to independent work. By providing structured support during guided practice, teachers create a safe learning environment where students can take risks, ask questions, and develop their skills incrementally, leading to a deeper and more lasting understanding of the material.

Impact	Preparation Time	Implementation Time
High	45 minutes	6–20 minutes

NEED IT	SEE IT	START IT	SHOW IT
Evidence shows . . .	Now: I will . . . Students will . . . Then: In three weeks' time, students will . . .	I will make this small, sustainable, and stackable by . . .	I will share my progress with . . .

PHASE 2: SURFACE WORKSHOP

Guided Practice

STEP 1

After you have demonstrated multiple examples of success, show students a new problem, and ask them to share the first steps with a partner. Make sure worked samples and criteria are out and are accessible for students.

STEP 2

Ask a number of students to share out the first step. Immediately show them your first step and connect your thinking to the success criteria. Once you identify student understanding, demonstrate the exact step and walk through the rationale for taking that step. Have students compare and contrast their approach to the problem with your approach.

STEP 3

Repeat step 2 for each step of the problem. Once you have completed each step of the problem, ask students to reflect on their successes and challenges.

STEP 4

Monitor the class for successes and challenges in meeting expectations. If 80% are proficient, move towards independent practice. If less than 80% reteach the concept and extend practice. Repeat steps 1-3 with new problems.

Numberless/Slow Reveal

A versatile learning activity applicable across various subjects and contexts, Numberless/Slow Reveal is designed to deepen students' engagement and comprehension. In the first read, students focus on gaining a general understanding of the text or word problem, familiarizing themselves with the main ideas and overall content. The second read shifts attention to specific details and comprehension questions, encouraging students to delve deeper into the material, identify key information, and clarify any uncertainties. During the third read, students engage in a more analytical approach, examining literary devices, themes, or the author's purpose. This iterative process not only enhances comprehension but also cultivates critical thinking and analytical skills. By systematically breaking down the text, the "3 Read" method ensures that students build a robust understanding, enabling them to apply their knowledge in varied contexts and fostering a more nuanced appreciation of the material.

Impact	Preparation Time	Implementation Time
High	15 minutes	20–25 minutes

NEED IT	SEE IT	START IT	SHOW IT
Evidence shows . . .	Now: I will . . . Students will . . . Then: In three weeks' time, students will . . .	I will make this small, sustainable, and stackable by . . .	I will share my progress with . . .

PHASE 2: SURFACE WORKSHOP

Numberless/ Slow Reveal

STEP 1

- Discuss and write down as a group what you know about the context of the problem.
- Ella bought __ apples and __ oranges. She ate __ apples and gave away __ oranges to Henry.
- The context is fruit.
- There are apples and oranges, some were eaten and some were given away.

Give students a word problem without the question or the numbers. Ask students to discuss and write down what they know about the context of the problem.

STEP 2

- What do we know now? What problems can be solved?
- Ella bought 12 apples and 8 oranges. She ate 3 apples and gave away 2 oranges to Henry.
- We need to take the 3 she ate away from the 12.
- If she gave 2 oranges away, we need to take 2 away from 8.

Provide students with the numbers and ask them to figure out what problems could be solved.

STEP 3

- Are we taking away oranges from apples?
- I see a subtraction problem we could solve.
- As a team, solve the problem and show your work. I will be doing the dots protocol to monitor our work.

Ask students to solve the problems they generated using what they learned from previous steps. Monitor student thinking and identify which groups are successful, which are close, and which are struggling. Then, present the actual problem and have students apply their insights to solve it.

STEP 4

- If you had a dot on your paper, you can attempt the new example. If you did not have a dot on your paper, I will do a mini workshop at the front table to provide support and answer questions.
- Ella bought 12 apples and 8 oranges. She ate 3 apples and gave away 2 oranges to Henry.

For students who successfully completed the problem, have them use different tool to solve the problem or give them a new problem. For students who are struggling to complete the problem, walk through the problem together using direct modeling approach.

Laib, J. (n.d.)

I Describe, You Draw

I Describe, You Draw is an engaging instructional strategy in which the teacher describes an object, scene, or concept, and students draw what they hear based on the description provided. This activity emphasizes listening skills, comprehension, and attention to detail, bridging the gap between verbal instructions and visual interpretation. As students listen to the teacher's detailed description, they must process the information accurately and translate it into a visual representation. This strategy not only enhances students' ability to follow directions but also encourages critical thinking and creativity. By comparing their drawings with the actual description, students can identify areas where their understanding may have diverged, leading to meaningful discussions and opportunities for clarification. Teachers can foster active participation while sharpening listening and comprehension skills, and promoting a collaborative, interactive learning environment where students learn to interpret and visualize complex information accurately.

Impact	Preparation Time	Implementation Time
High	5 minutes	15–20 minutes

NEED IT	SEE IT	START IT	SHOW IT
Evidence shows . . .	Now: I will . . . Students will . . . Then: In three weeks' time, students will . . .	I will make this small, sustainable, and stackable by . . .	I will share my progress with . . .

PHASE 2: SURFACE WORKSHOP

I Describe, You Draw

STEP 1

Pair students to sit back-to-back. One student receives a card with a shape or diagram on it. Without showing the card, they must describe the shape in detail using only words. The other student listens and attempts to draw the shape on a blank paper based soley on the verbal instructions.

STEP 2

After students complete the drawing, have partners compare the original and drawn shapes and discuss the accuracy of communication and the role of precise academic language.

STEP 3

Have Student A give instructions on how to draw the image on the paper using academic vocabulary. Have Student B draw the image.

STEP 4

Debrief the two iterations and discuss the power of using academic vocabulary. Repeat Steps 1-4 with the partners switching roles.

Phase 3: Deep Workshop Overview

In the third phase of rigorous project-based learning (PBL), students move beyond foundational knowledge to develop a deep understanding of core disciplinary ideas. This phase prioritizes analytical thinking, argumentation, and the ability to relate and apply concepts across different contexts. Students refine their ability to compare and contrast ideas through protocols like the Venn Diagram and 2 Box Induction, which help them examine similarities, differences, and relationships between key concepts.

Deep learning also requires students to develop skills in argumentation and persuasion. The Four A's Protocol and SPAR (Spontaneous Argumentation) encourage students to critically engage with texts, debate perspectives, and support their claims with evidence. These strategies not only strengthen their reasoning and communication skills but also prepare them for real-world applications of discourse and problem-solving.

To ensure students are connecting deep learning to both prior surface-level knowledge and future transfer-level application, teachers guide them in using structured tools such as the Frayer Model and In2Out Protocol. These strategies help students refine definitions, categorize ideas, and align their understanding with the project's overall expectations. By continuously linking deep learning to both foundational knowledge and broader project goals, students develop a comprehensive, interconnected understanding that prepares them for meaningful application and synthesis in the final phase of PBL.

Impact	Preparation Time	Implementation Time
High	45 minutes	6–20 minutes

NEED IT	SEE IT	START IT	SHOW IT
Evidence shows . . .	Now: I will . . . Students will . . . Then: In three weeks' time, students will . . .	I will make this small, sustainable, and stackable by . . .	I will share my progress with . . .

PHASE 3: DEEP LEARNING

Deep Workshop Overview

STEP 1

Introduce a strategy that engages students in analyzing and applying key ideas, skills, and processes through reading, writing, and discussion. Guide them to compare, contrast, and identify cause-and-effect relationships. As you model the process, highlight patterns between ideas and encourage students to ask "why" and "how" questions to move beyond memorization and deepen their understanding.

STEP 2

Guide students through a thinking routine or protocol that builds conceptual understanding by prompting analysis and synthesis. Ask open-ended questions that connect multiple ideas, skills, and processes, and use misconception checks to identify and correct faulty reasoning.

STEP 3

Lead structured group activities where students apply concepts using claims, evidence, and reasoning. Encourage them to debate different perspectives, make connections across subjects, and use formative assessments to deepen inquiry and strengthen understanding.

STEP 4

Have students deepen their understanding by applying concepts across subjects through reading, writing and discussion. Support them in connecting key ideas, defending or challenging reasoning, and critically evaluating the thinking of peers, authors, and different perspectives.

Venn Diagram

A Venn Diagram is a valuable tool for helping students visually organize and compare information. The process begins by introducing the concepts or topics to be analyzed, then setting up overlapping circles, each labeled with one of the topics. Students list unique characteristics of each concept in the non-overlapping parts and place shared characteristics in the overlapping sections. This exercise helps students identify both differences and similarities, reinforcing comprehension and encouraging connections between ideas. A class discussion can follow to deepen understanding, and students can then apply their insights through related assignments. Venn Diagrams foster critical thinking and are especially effective for compare-and-contrast activities across subjects.

Impact	Preparation Time	Implementation Time
High	5 minutes	20–30 minutes

NEED IT	SEE IT	START IT	SHOW IT
Evidence shows . . .	Now: I will . . . Students will . . . Then: In three weeks' time, students will . . .	I will make this small, sustainable, and stackable by . . .	I will share my progress with . . .

PHASE 3: DEEP LEARNING

Venn Diagram

STEP 1

Present a stimulus, idea, or standard and work with students to identify similarities in the middle of a Venn Diagram. The Venn Diagram provides a means for identifying commonalities and differences across topics.

STEP 2

Work with students to examine the two outside sections of the Venn Diagram. Guide them in identifying unique characteristics or examples specific to each category. Encourage them to justify why these features belong exclusively in one circle and not the overlapping middle. Use probing questions to deepen analysis and help students refine their reasoning.

STEP 3

Have students work together to build off of the class designed Venn Diagram.

STEP 4

To ensure students understand the content, have students share their ideas with the class. When necessary, provide corrective feedback.

2 Box Induction

The 2 Box Induction strategy involves analyzing two contrasting examples or concepts within a larger topic, helping students build a deeper understanding through focused comparison. By identifying key characteristics, similarities, and differences, students gain insights into the overall category being studied. This process not only enhances their analytical skills but also aids in building and refining hypotheses and models. As students test their initial ideas against different pieces of evidence, they place these ideas in the appropriate box based on their viability. This iterative process of testing, comparing, and refining leads to a more nuanced and comprehensive understanding of the concepts. 2 Box Induction encourages critical thinking and promotes an active learning environment where students continuously evaluate and adjust their understanding, resulting in a more sophisticated grasp of the subject matter.

Impact	Preparation Time	Implementation Time
High	15 minutes	10–15 minutes

NEED IT	SEE IT	START IT	SHOW IT
Evidence shows . . .	Now: I will . . . Students will . . . Then: In three weeks' time, students will . . .	I will make this small, sustainable, and stackable by . . .	I will share my progress with . . .

PHASE 3: DEEP LEARNING

2 Box Induction

STEP 1

Present two boxes and share that students will need to find the pattern found across each box.

STEP 2

Show students the first item in each box and ask students to discuss the similarities and differences with a peer. Randomly check responses and write them down as "hunches" on the board. Provide cues for forming complex sentences (e.g., because, but, and so).

STEP 3

Repeat this process by slowly showing concepts in both boxes. Ensure students are discussing similarities and differences within and across each box. Continue to randomly check students predictions.

STEP 4

Ask students to predict the key theme/text/rule/pattern in each box. Provide the actual rule and ask students to reflect on their predictions.

4 A's Protocol

The 4A's is a text protocol used for analyzing and discussing texts in a collaborative and engaging way. It focuses on four key perspectives:

Assumptions: Students identify the underlying assumptions and biases presented in the text. This includes examining the author's perspective, cultural context, and potential hidden agendas.

Agreements: Students discuss and identify the points of agreement they find in the text. This helps them build consensus and focus on shared understanding.

Arguments: Students analyze the arguments presented in the text, identifying evidence, reasoning, and potential fallacies. This encourages critical thinking and evaluation of ideas.

Aspirations: Students consider the text's implications and potential impact. They discuss how the text relates to their own values, goals, and aspirations for the future.

Impact	Preparation Time	Implementation Time
High	5 minutes	15–30 minutes

Source: National School Reform Faculty, 2017.

NEED IT	SEE IT	START IT	SHOW IT
Evidence shows . . .	Now: I will . . . Students will . . . Then: In three weeks' time, students will . . .	I will make this small, sustainable, and stackable by . . .	I will share my progress with . . .

PHASE 3: DEEP LEARNING

Four A's Protocol

STEP 1

Present students with four questions they will attempt to answer as they read a passage. Those questions include:
Assumptions- What are the assumptions the author of the text holds?
Argue- What do you disagree with in this text?
Agree- What do you agree with in this text?
Aspire- What do you aspire to after reading this text?

STEP 2

After students have finished reading the text, organize them into small groups. Instruct groups to work through the 4 A's questions in order, discussing and answering one question at a time before moving to the next. Emphasize the importance of building on each response to deepen understanding and ensure that all group members contribute to each answer.

STEP 3

As groups work through the questions, monitor their discussions to ensure they are addressing all parts of the 4 A's. If a group skips an "A" or rushes through, pause them and guide them back to fully explore that step. Take notes on common patterns to bring up in the class debrief.

STEP 4

Lead a classroom discussion where students share what they agree and disagree with in the text, focusing specifically on the author's assumptions and underlying messages. Invite students to share their own aspirations or hopes after engaging with the text. Use probing questions to prompt students to cite evidence, strengthen their reasoning, and deepen the overall discussion.

SPAR (Spontaneous Argumentation)

The SPAR (Spontaneous Argumentation) workshop is an interactive instructional strategy that hones students' critical thinking and debating skills by engaging them in impromptu arguments. This process begins with the teacher presenting a controversial topic or question, which students then address in a spontaneous debate format. Participants are typically divided into two opposing sides, with each side having limited preparation time to develop their arguments. Students must think quickly, articulate their points clearly, and respond to counterarguments effectively. This workshop emphasizes the importance of evidence-based reasoning, encouraging students to support their positions with relevant facts and logical arguments. By participating in SPAR, students enhance their ability to think on their feet, improve their public speaking skills, and learn to engage respectfully and constructively with differing viewpoints. The SPAR workshop fosters a dynamic and engaging learning environment, promoting active participation and deeper understanding of the subject matter through spontaneous, real-time argumentation.

Impact	Preparation Time	Implementation Time
High	5 minutes	15–30 minutes

Source: Facing History, n.d

NEED IT	SEE IT	START IT	SHOW IT
Evidence shows . . .	Now: I will . . . Students will . . . Then: In three weeks' time, students will . . .	I will make this small, sustainable, and stackable by . . .	I will share my progress with . . .

PHASE 3: DEEP LEARNING

SPAR (Spontaneous Argumentation)

STEP 1
Have students form alternative opinions to an argumentative question on the board.

STEP 2
Assign students to a particular position and have them stand on opposite sides of the classroom. Have each group discuss claims, evidence and reasoning for the assigned opinion.

STEP 3
Students pair up with someone assigned the opposite position and each student presents their argument, resulting in a spontaneous debate.

STEP 4
Reform the groups in Step 2 and have them create a 1-minute concluding statement that attempts to either counter the opposing views or find a way to combine the views to find a solution that connects differing perspectives. If time permits, have students reflect on the process and how this helped them or hindered them in understanding various perspectives on an issue.

Frayer Model

The Frayer Model is a graphic organizer designed to help students delve deeper into the meaning of a concept. This model typically consists of four boxes structured as follows: the top-left box contains the definition of the concept, providing a clear and concise explanation. The top-right box includes examples of the concept in action, illustrating its application in various contexts. The bottom-left box features non-examples to clarify what the concept is not, helping to eliminate misconceptions and differentiate it from similar ideas. The bottom-right box lists characteristics that define the concept, highlighting its essential attributes and features. By organizing information in this manner, the Frayer Model enables students to comprehensively explore and understand the concept, facilitating critical thinking and retention. This structured approach not only deepens comprehension but also enhances the ability to apply the concept accurately in different scenarios, promoting a more robust and enduring grasp of the subject matter.

Impact	Preparation Time	Implementation Time
High	5 minutes	15–30 minutes

Source: Frayer et al., 1969.

NEED IT	SEE IT	START IT	SHOW IT
Evidence shows . . .	Now: I will . . . Students will . . . Then: In three weeks' time, students will . . .	I will make this small, sustainable, and stackable by . . .	I will share my progress with . . .

PHASE 3: DEEP LEARNING

Frayer Model

STEP 1

Present the Frayer Model and ask students to discuss their confidence in solving each problem.

STEP 2

Task students with completing the square that fits their confidence level.

STEP 3

Pair up students who solved the same problem and have them discuss their ideas, provide feedback, and make any necessary adjustments to their initial responses.

STEP 4

Place students into groups of four, with each student representing one square of the model, and have them discuss their answers. Then, check the answers and return to the original question. This process should bring together students from with varying confidence levels to discuss their findings, verify their answers, and collectively address the original problem.

In2Out Protocol

The In2Out Protocol (*In* = individual, *2* = partner share, *Out* = group discussion) emphasizes transitioning from personal understanding ("In") to broader perspectives and group discussion ("Out"). This protocol typically begins with individual reflection, where students contemplate their own understanding and experiences related to a topic. The prompt can then change and students discuss the new prompt with a partner in the room. Following this partner share, students share their personal insights and experiences with the group, fostering a richer, more diverse dialogue. Constructive questioning is then employed to challenge assumptions, clarify ideas, and delve deeper into the subject matter. Finally, the analysis of different viewpoints allows students to synthesize various perspectives, broadening their understanding and promoting collaborative learning. The In2Out Protocol not only enhances individual comprehension but also cultivates a more inclusive and dynamic learning environment, where students learn to appreciate and integrate multiple viewpoints, leading to a more nuanced and comprehensive grasp of the topic.

Impact	Preparation Time	Implementation Time
High	10 minutes	30–40 minutes

Source: San Francisco Coalition of Essential Small Schools, 2019.

NEED IT	SEE IT	START IT	SHOW IT
Evidence shows . . .	Now: I will . . . Students will . . . Then: In three weeks' time, students will . . .	I will make this small, sustainable, and stackable by . . .	I will share my progress with . . .

PHASE 3: DEEP LEARNING

In 2 Out Protocol

STEP 1

Begin by having students read a text. Provide a short prompt for students to silently reflect on in a journal. They keep their responses private in this "inside" phase.

STEP 2

Begin the "2" portion of the protocol by placing students in pairs and presenting them with a new question. Circulate the room and listen to student responses.

STEP 3

Begin the "out" portion by placing students in a circle and providing a new prompt. Students should each state their ideas going clockwise. If a student wants to pass they may. After the group completes the discussion, go back to those students that passed and ask them to either share their own idea or paraphrase what someone else said.

STEP 4

Encourage students to articulate how their thinking evolved during the "In2Out protocol". Encourage students to build on other's thoughts and validate other's perspectives.

Phase 4 - Project Conclusion and Reflection

In the fourth and final phase of rigorous project-based learning (PBL), students move into transfer-level learning, applying their knowledge and skills beyond the initial context. This phase challenges them to engage in complex problem-solving, adapt to new challenges, and refine their ability to think critically across different situations.

Students begin by tackling problems within familiar contexts using protocols like the 3 C's, which prompt them to consider challenges, choices, and consequences. They then extend their thinking across disciplines using Jigsaw, allowing them to synthesize ideas and make interdisciplinary connections.

Handling setbacks and feedback is essential in this phase. Protocols such as Red Team and Situation Room challenge students to anticipate obstacles, refine arguments, and adjust solutions based on constructive critique. Friendly Controversy encourages them to engage in meaningful discussions, weigh perspectives, and defend their reasoning—building resilience and adaptability for real-world problem-solving.

Finally, students present their work and insights through strategies like the Gallery Walk, showcasing their thinking, engaging in peer review, and reflecting on the learning process. This culminating phase reinforces their ability to apply knowledge in novel situations and prepares them to navigate complex, real-life challenges with confidence and creativity.

Impact	Preparation Time	Implementation Time
High	10 minutes	30–40 minutes

NEED IT	SEE IT	START IT	SHOW IT
Evidence shows . . .	Now: I will . . . Students will . . . Then: In three weeks' time, students will . . .	I will make this small, sustainable, and stackable by . . .	I will share my progress with . . .

PHASE 4: PROJECT CONCLUSION AND REFLECTION

Project Reflection/Conclusion

STEP 1

Have students work in small groups to identify the key content they need to include in their responses to the driving question. Encourage them to focus on the most important concepts and information that support a strong accurate response.

STEP 2

Ask students to identify common themes and unique differences across multiple contexts. Guide them to connect surface knowledge and deep understanding to transfer-level thinking by analyzing how key ideas appear or change in different situations. Have students compare their solutions and reasoning with others to deepend their understanding and refine their ideas.

STEP 3

Have students present their selected solutions to the problem and engage with feedback from peers, teachers, or experts. Encourage them to reflect on challenges that arise, respond to unexpected questions or changes, and consider how their solution might evolve or lead to a next phase of work.

STEP 4

Ask students to reflect on how their thinking, skills and understanding have grown throughout the project. Encourage them to provide specific examples of what they learned and how they improved.

3 C's

The 3 C's transfer workshop is an instructional strategy where students use multiple perspectives to analyze a topic, theme, or subject. This workshop encourages students to explore various assumptions and viewpoints, including those from marginalized groups, to gain a comprehensive understanding of the issue at hand. Through this process, students critically examine different perspectives, challenging their own assumptions and biases. By integrating diverse viewpoints, they develop more accurate and nuanced responses to complex dilemmas. The 3 C's fosters empathy, critical thinking, and inclusivity, promoting a deeper appreciation for the richness of multiple perspectives. This method not only enhances students' analytical skills but also prepares them to approach real-world problems with a more informed and balanced viewpoint, leading to more thoughtful and equitable solutions.

Impact	Preparation Time	Implementation Time
High	10 minutes	20–25 minutes

NEED IT	SEE IT	START IT	SHOW IT
Evidence shows . . .	Now: I will . . . Students will . . . Then: In three weeks' time, students will . . .	I will make this small, sustainable, and stackable by . . .	I will share my progress with . . .

PHASE 4: PROJECT CONCLUSION AND REFLECTION

3 C's

STEP 1

Critical

Speech bubbles: "What is the overall summary from the text?" / "The text is saying..."

The teacher asks students to review a summary on a topic (e.g., an AI generated summary, newspaper article, textbook). They are expected to evaluate the summary using classroom resources, learning intentions and success criteria.
Questions may include:
- What is the overall summary from the text?
- What is the main idea?
- To what extent is the information valid and reliable?

STEP 2

Critically

Speech bubbles: "What perspectives are missing, especially from marginalized communities?" / "This text is only showing one perspective..." / "I wonder if we could find a different view of this issue?"

The teacher prompts students to evaluate the effectiveness or use of multiple perspectives in the analysis.
Questions might include:
- What assumptions are present in this passage?
- Which perspectives, particularly those from marginalized communities, are missing?
- What additional viewpoints could enhance our understanding of the situation?

STEP 3

Contribution

Speech bubbles: "How should we write about this topic?" / "We need to share with the audience the limitations of each resource." / "We need to include multiple voices."

The teacher asks students to determine ways they could contribute to the accuracy and future prospect of the summary (e.g., questions to ask, problems to solve).
Questions may include:
- What questions should we ask/answer?
- How should we write/speak about this topic?
- What actions can/should we take to improve the accuracy and scope of the information?

STEP 4

Reflection

Speech bubbles: "What did we learn from this process?" / "I learned that the accuracy of one source is only a part of the puzzle." / "I learned that bias is hard to detect."

The teacher asks students to share their responses to the class across each step. This is an opportunity for teachers to work with students to discuss how this process can be used when reading texts and studying other topics.

Jigsaw

Jigsaw is a cooperative learning strategy designed to promote deeper understanding and collaboration among students. With this method, students first become experts on a specific topic or section of the material. They then regroup into mixed groups where each member shares their expertise, collectively piecing together a comprehensive understanding of the overall subject. Throughout the session, students rotate through different stations or locations in the room, synthesizing the information they receive from each "expert" at the previous station. This dynamic process not only enhances individual knowledge but also fosters a sense of interdependence and teamwork. By relying on each other's expertise, students develop communication and teaching skills, deepen their grasp of the material, and learn to appreciate the value of diverse perspectives. The Jigsaw process creates an engaging and interactive learning environment, encouraging active participation and ensuring that all students contribute to and benefit from the collective learning experience.

Impact	Preparation Time	Implementation Time
High	20 minutes	45–55 minutes

NEED IT	SEE IT	START IT	SHOW IT
Evidence shows . . .	Now: I will . . . Students will . . . Then: In three weeks' time, students will . . .	I will make this small, sustainable, and stackable by . . .	I will share my progress with . . .

PHASE 4: PROJECT CONCLUSION AND REFLECTION

Jigsaw

STEP 1

Assign students to small groups and give each group a specific portion of the text to read and analyze. Instruct them to identify key ideas, summarize their section, and prepare a short presentation to teach other groups or the rest of the class what they learned. Encourage them to include important quotes, connections to earlier content, and questions for discussions.

STEP 2

Once groups have read their portion of the text, have them answer a set of probing questions to make sure they're ready to present the information. Have them work on answering surface, deep and transfer questions.

STEP 3

Regroup students so that each group has someone who is an "expert" for each portion of the text. Ask each person to share their learning including their answers to the surface, deep and transfer questions.

STEP 4

Ask the entire class a series of questions to make sure they have a thorough understanding of the material and how each compenent relates to one another.

Red Team

The Red Team is designed to enhance critical thinking and problem-solving skills by having students adopt an adversarial perspective. Students are divided into "red teams," tasked with challenging ideas, strategies, or solutions presented by their peers, effectively playing the role of a devil's advocate. The process involves scrutinizing assumptions, identifying potential flaws, and proposing alternative viewpoints. The Red Team strategy not only improves analytical and debating skills but also fosters a culture of open-mindedness and resilience. Students learn to anticipate counterarguments, refine their reasoning, and strengthen their ability to defend their positions. This method encourages a collaborative, yet challenging, learning environment where critical feedback is valued and leveraged to enhance overall understanding and innovation.

Impact	Preparation Time	Implementation Time
High	10 minutes	20–30 minutes

NEED IT	SEE IT	START IT	SHOW IT
Evidence shows . . .	Now: I will . . . Students will . . . Then: In three weeks' time, students will . . .	I will make this small, sustainable, and stackable by . . .	I will share my progress with . . .

PHASE 4: PROJECT CONCLUSION AND REFLECTION

Red Team

STEP 1

Organize the class into two problem-soving groups facing each other, labeled Group A (for) and Group B (against).

STEP 2

Have Group A present their solution to Group B. Then, instruct Group B to ask clarifying questions. Group A should listen and respond to the questions thoughtfully.

STEP 3

Ask Group B to share a series of "I wonder" statements (e.g. I wonder if other solutions or perspectives were considered? I wonder if variable A changes how this solution will work?). Instruct Group A to listen without responding.

STEP 4

Have Group A reflect aloud on Group B's "I wonder" questions while Group B listens silently. Then, switch roles so Group B presents their solution and the same process is repeated. Let students know that they will use the Red Team protocol again later in the unit to give feedback on their own work, so this round is also practice for applying to future assignments, projects, and presentations.

Situation Room

The Situation Room is an interactive strategy that challenges students to analyze scenarios, generate creative solutions, and refine their ideas through discussion and collaboration. Students begin by working with a partner to interpret a given scenario, ensuring they understand the task. They then join new groups to exchange ideas and explore different possibilities, expanding their perspectives through shared brainstorming. After gathering insights, students return to their original groups to refine their approach and decide on the best course of action. Finally, teams present their revised ideas to the class, sharing their creative decisions and reasoning. This process encourages active engagement, flexible thinking, and meaningful discussion while strengthening problem-solving and communication skills.

Impact	Preparation Time	Implementation Time
High	5 minutes	35–45 minutes

NEED IT	SEE IT	START IT	SHOW IT
Evidence shows . . .	Now: I will . . . Students will . . . Then: In three weeks' time, students will . . .	I will make this small, sustainable, and stackable by . . .	I will share my progress with . . .

PHASE 4: PROJECT CONCLUSION AND REFLECTION

Situation Room

STEP 1

Place students in pairs or small groups and provide them with a variety of new scenarios or situations. These changes may include small changes to their current work, such as a slight change in their tasks or could be a major change in a problem they are working on. The degree of changes should be based on their current understanding of surface and deep content.

STEP 2

Next, pair students with new partners to debrief their current approach to their respective situation. Give each pair about four minutes to share their scenarios and next steps (approximately two minutes per students). Afterward, lead a brief class discussion on common approaches to addressing the situations.

STEP 3

Have students return to their original pairs and begin planning how they will address the scenario. Let them know they will share their ideas with the class in less than 10 minutes.

STEP 4

Have students share their ideas and discuss what changes they made during the last three steps.

Friendly Controversy

The Friendly Controversy process is where students explain and defend their positions on topics about which they disagree, following specific guidelines to ensure respectful and constructive dialogue. The teacher sets clear guidelines that encourage students to engage in controversy, while emphasizing respect, active listening, and open-mindedness. Students are encouraged to express their opinions freely while acknowledging and considering opposing viewpoints. This process fosters a safe environment for intellectual exchange, where students learn to articulate their arguments clearly, support their positions with evidence, and listen attentively to others. Sentence stems and frames are a way to scaffold the conversation. By practicing respectful disagreement, students develop critical thinking, empathy, and communication skills. This method encourages students to approach disagreements as opportunities for growth and learning, ultimately leading to more well-rounded and informed viewpoints.

Impact	Preparation Time	Implementation Time
High	15–20 minutes	25–40 minutes

NEED IT	SEE IT	START IT	SHOW IT
Evidence shows . . .	Now: I will . . . Students will . . . Then: In three weeks' time, students will . . .	I will make this small, sustainable, and stackable by . . .	I will share my progress with . . .

PHASE 4: PROJECT CONCLUSION AND REFLECTION

Friendly Controversy

STEP 1

"Let's list a number of viewpoints that should be considered when thinking about our driving question. With each viewpoint let's discuss any evidence we have to back up those ideas."

Should we correct all of the misspelled words in the U.S. Constitution?

"One viewpoint is that if we begin changing words we may begin to change ideas. That could be scary."

"Pennsylvania is misspelled. This can be observed by actually reading the document. We should change that."

Present the driving question and illustrate a number of viewpoints that are found within this question. Share with students that the point here is to explain their perspective with evidence and to listen to others.

STEP 2

"We are about to engage in a bit of friendly controversy. The key is to focus on ideas not people. For instance, when you critique, I want you to say 'The idea that...' versus 'Your idea is...'"

Should we correct all of the misspelled words in the U.S. Constitution?

Share ground rules including "critiquing ideas not people." Provide an example and then ask students to generate an example.

STEP 3

"Let's begin the protocol by having someone in the class share their opinion and cite evidence, if possible, on making a change to the Constitution."

Should we correct all of the misspelled words in the U.S. Constitution?

"This is a quick fix. They have over 600 misspellings from the class research. Are there other opinions?"

Person one shares their opinion, cites evidence, and then asks a question about the viewpoints of others.

STEP 4

"Let's continue by having someone in the class counter this idea."

Should we correct all of the misspelled words in the U.S. Constitution?

"The idea sounds simple, but the constitution hasn't changed since the early '90s due to lack of votes. Are there other perspectives?"

Next, person 2 shares their opinion, evidence, and questions. This process should be repeated multiple times.

Marzano, R.J. (2016)

Gallery Walk

The Gallery Walk process is an interactive strategy where students display their work at various spots around the classroom, allowing their peers to move around and explore the learning materials posted at different stations. This method encourages students to engage with each other's work actively, making observations and drawing insights as they circulate the room. After exploring the displayed work, students discuss their observations and insights with each other, providing constructive feedback in a structured format, typically using prompts such as "I like . . .," "I wonder . . .," and "A next step might be . . ." The Gallery Walk process fosters a dynamic and collaborative learning environment, promoting critical thinking and reflective dialogue. It allows students to appreciate diverse approaches and perspectives, enhances their ability to give and receive feedback, and encourages continuous improvement and deeper understanding through peer interaction and discussion. This method not only validates students' efforts but also cultivates a sense of community and shared learning.

Impact	Preparation Time	Implementation Time
High	5 minutes	35–45 minutes

NEED IT	SEE IT	START IT	SHOW IT
Evidence shows . . .	Now: I will . . . Students will . . . Then: In three weeks' time, students will . . .	I will make this small, sustainable, and stackable by . . .	I will share my progress with . . .

PHASE 4: PROJECT CONCLUSION AND REFLECTION

Gallery Walk

STEP 1

Gather all of the project ideas from your students. This could be in the form of posters, presentations, or digital artifacts. Display the project ideas around the classroom, giving each project a designated space. Create a handout for students to use during the gallery walk. This handout should include the learning intentions and success criteria for the project, as well as some questions to help students guide their discussion.

STEP 2

Tell students that the purpose of the gallery walk is to give content-focused feedback that helps their classmates improve their work. Have students review the learning intention, success criteria, and sentence starters so they are prepared to give specific, helpful feedback to peers.
For example:
    I like how you have met the success criteria by _____?
    I wonder if you have considered _____?
    A next step might be _____?

STEP 3

Conduct the gallery walk in a quiet room to ensure students share their own thoughts. Give students a set amount of time to provide written feedback on a post-it note to place on the poster.

STEP 4

Have students review the feedback on their poster and determine next steps. Have students share our their next steps with the class.

Conclusion

THE STRATEGIES IN THIS BOOK are designed to bring consistency and precision to instructional practice, ensuring that every routine aligns with the right learning phase for maximum impact. Teaching is not about guesswork; it's about refining habits, sequencing learning experiences with clarity, and maintaining structured, repeatable approaches that drive student growth. By committing to deliberate practice and avoiding variability in implementation, we can shift PBL from an inconsistent experience to a highly predictable, effective, and transformative method of instruction.

The true rocket science of teaching, and rigorous PBL is no exception, is consistency and precision; it's not in complexity, but in the degree to which we refine and sustain our practices. This book is more than a resource; it is a blueprint for disciplined action. Whether you are a teacher embedding high-impact strategies, a PLC refining instructional routines, or a coach guiding professional growth, the key lies in small, deliberate adjustments that, over time, create significant learning gains. The power of nuance—the precise timing of a question, the structure of a scaffold, or the sequence of a routine—can make the difference between superficial engagement and meaningful mastery.

As you move forward, embrace the discipline of consistency and the rigor of precision. Teaching is not about constant reinvention—it is about refining what works, making small but meaningful shifts, and ensuring every instructional move is intentional. By doing so, we create a learning experience where students experience the depth, clarity, and transferability of knowledge they need to succeed. When this occurs, we find PBL that not only provides real-world, authentic experiences but also ensures rigorous learning. This will prepare students for the opportunities and challenges ahead.

As you have seen, this book is an exceptional resource for strengthening surface, deep, and transfer learning, but you don't have to take this journey alone. Invite Michael, Aaron, or one of their teammates to your school or system by contacting us at info@mimitoddpress.com.

References

Brooks, D. (2024). You might be a late bloomer. *The Atlantic.* Retrieved from https://www.theatlantic.com/ideas/archive/2024/06/successs-late-bloomers-motivation/678798/

Claxton, G. (2019). *The learning power approach: Teaching learners to teach themselves.* Crown House Publishing.

Facing History. (n.d.). *SPAR: Spontaneous argumentation.* Retrieved from https://www.facinghistory.org/resource-library/spar-spontaneous-argumentation

Frayer, D. A., Frederick, W. C., & Klausmeier, H. J. (1969). *A schema for testing the level of concept mastery.* Wisconsin Center for Education Research.

Hattie, J. (2009). *Visible learning: A synthesis of over 800 meta-analyses relating to achievement.* Routledge.

Hattie, J. (2023). *Visible learning: The sequel.* Routledge.

Hattie, J., & Donoghue, G. (2016). Learning strategies: A synthesis and conceptual model. *Educational Psychology Review, 28*(2), 207–234.

Laib, J. (n.d.). Slow reveal graphs. https://slowrevealgraphs.com

Marzano, R. J. (2016). Using friendly controversy. Marzano Research. https://pcmslookforsmarzano.wordpress.com/wp-content/uploads/2017/08/usingfriendlycontroversy.pdf

National School Reform Faculty. (2017). *Four A's text protocol.* Retrieved from https://www.nsrfharmony.org/wp-content/uploads/2017/10/FourAsTextProtocol-N.pdf

Rosenshine, B. (2012). Principles of instruction: Research-based strategies that all teachers should know. *American Educator, 36*(1), 12–19.

San Francisco Coalition of Essential Small Schools. (2019). *Using SF-CESS discourse cards.* Retrieved from https://sfcess.org/wp-content/uploads/2019/02/Usiing-SF-CESS-Discourse-Cards.pdf

Sherrington, T., & Goodwin, D. (2022). Five Ways One-Pagers Booklet 1 [PDF]. Teacherhead. https://teacherhead.com/wp-content/uploads/2022/09/five-ways-one-pagers-booklet-1.pdf

Glossary

4 A's Protocol – A structured text analysis strategy where students explore a text through four key perspectives: Assumptions, Agreements, Arguments, and Aspirations to develop critical thinking and deeper comprehension.

3 C's – A reflective strategy prompting students to consider Challenges, Choices, and Consequences when analyzing problems or decision-making processes.

Agency, Student – The ability of students to take ownership of their learning by making choices, setting goals, and engaging in self-directed learning experiences.

Assessment Scramble – A pre-assessment method that presents students with scrambled questions or tasks to identify initial knowledge, misunderstandings, and areas for deeper inquiry.

Backwards Design – A planning framework that begins with defining desired learning outcomes and then developing instructional activities and assessments to achieve those outcomes.

Culturally Responsive Teaching (CRT) – Instruction that recognizes and incorporates students' cultural backgrounds to make learning more relevant and effective.

Clues Approach – A collaborative learning method where students and teachers co-construct learning intentions and success criteria, using formative assessment to refine learning goals.

Collaborative Learning – An instructional approach in which students work together to achieve shared learning goals, emphasizing communication and cooperation.

Collaborative Professional Learning – A professional development approach that involves educators working together to identify, implement, and refine effective teaching practices.

Compass Points – A critical thinking routine where students examine a topic from multiple perspectives: Excited (E), Worrisome (W), Need to Know (N), and Stance/Suggestion (S).

Comparing Work Samples – A strategy where students analyze exemplar work samples to identify quality indicators, compare their own work, and refine their understanding of success criteria.

Competency-Based Learning (CBL) – An educational approach where students progress based on demonstrating mastery of specific skills or knowledge rather than time spent in class.

Competency-Based Habits – Learning behaviors that help students develop knowledge at surface, deep, and transfer levels, supporting long-term mastery and application of skills.

Constructivist Learning – A learning theory that emphasizes the learner's active role in constructing knowledge through experiences, reflection, and social interaction.

Consultancy Dilemma – A structured process where students or educators present a problem or challenge and receive peer feedback through clarifying questions and suggested solutions.

Critical Pedagogy – An educational philosophy advocating for the empowerment of learners through questioning and challenging dominant narratives and structures.

Critical Thinking – The process of analyzing, evaluating, and synthesizing information to form reasoned judgments.

Deep Learning – The process of developing meaningful connections between concepts, emphasizing analytical thinking, reasoning, and application of knowledge across different contexts.

Differentiated Instruction – Adapting instruction to meet the diverse learning needs, readiness levels, and interests of students.

Dispositional Learning – The development of mindsets, behaviors, and skills that enable students to become self-directed, reflective, and adaptive learners.

Dispositional Strategies – Techniques that help students develop habits of thinking, including metacognition, perseverance, collaboration, and self-assessment.

Empathy Protocol – A strategy designed to help students develop an awareness of others' perspectives and experiences to foster compassion and inclusivity.

Error Analysis – A method where students examine mistakes in their work to understand misconceptions and refine their learning processes.

Essential Question – Open-ended questions that drive inquiry and focus learning on core themes or concepts.

Feedback Loop – A continuous cycle of providing and receiving feedback to refine learning processes and improve outcomes.

Fishbone Diagram – A visual tool used to identify the root causes of a problem, organizing contributing factors in a structured way.

Formative Assessment – Ongoing assessments designed to monitor student learning and provide actionable feedback for instructional adjustments.

Frayer Model – A graphic organizer with four quadrants used to define a concept, provide examples and non-examples, and list key characteristics.

Gallery Walk – An interactive strategy where students display their work around the classroom and engage in peer review and reflection through structured movement and discussion.

Gradual Release of Responsibility (GRR) – An instructional model that shifts from teacher-led instruction to independent student practice through stages: "I Do, We Do, You Do."

Green and Red – A strategy in which students use green or red indicators to communicate their level of understanding in real time, allowing teachers to provide immediate support.

Guided Practice – A scaffolded instructional approach where teachers provide direct support and feedback as students develop proficiency in new skills or concepts.

Headlines – A summarization technique in which students create concise, impactful statements that capture the essence of their learning.

Hot Seat – A discussion strategy where one person presents a challenge, and the group listens, asks clarifying questions, and collaboratively generates solutions.

Inquiry-Based Learning (IBL) – A student-centered approach where learning is driven by questioning, exploration, and investigation of real-world problems.

In2Out Protocol – A structured discussion process where students move from individual reflection (In), to partner discussion (2), to whole-class conversation (Out) to deepen understanding.

Jigsaw – A cooperative learning strategy where students become experts on different aspects of a topic and share their knowledge in mixed groups to build collective understanding.

KWL Chart – A graphic organizer that helps students identify what they already **K**now, what they **W**ant to learn, and what they have **L**earned about a topic.

Known, Nuance, and Novel – A reflection strategy where students categorize their understanding into what they already know, what is nuanced or slightly different, and what is completely new.

Matrix Problems – A problem-solving routine where students analyze patterns, relationships, and structures across different scenarios to develop analytical thinking skills.

Metacognition – The process of thinking about one's own thinking, involving self-awareness, monitoring, and regulating learning strategies.

Opinion Lines – A discussion strategy where students position themselves along a continuum from "Strongly Agree" to "Strongly Disagree" and justify their reasoning.

Perspective Analysis – The examination of multiple viewpoints on a topic to develop a deeper understanding and appreciation of different perspectives.

PLCs (Professional Learning Communities) – Groups of educators who collaborate to analyze student data, refine teaching practices, and improve student learning outcomes.

Question Before Comments – A discussion routine that encourages students to ask clarifying questions before making evaluative statements about a topic or idea.

Rapid Writing – A timed writing activity where students continuously write on a topic to improve fluency and generate ideas.

Reciprocal Teaching – A student-led discussion strategy that rotates roles, including questioning, summarizing, clarifying, and predicting, to enhance reading comprehension.

Reflection – The practice of thinking critically about one's learning experiences, progress, and areas for improvement.

Semantic Webbing – A visual strategy that helps students organize and connect related ideas in a web-like structure to deepen understanding.

Shadow Protocol – A structured observational process where students analyze peer interactions and learning behaviors without participating.

Sticky Note Protocol – A peer feedback technique in which students provide warm and cool feedback on their classmates' work using sticky notes.

Surface Learning – The foundational level of learning that focuses on acquiring basic knowledge, facts, and procedures.

GLOSSARY

Sustainable Practices – Instructional approaches that are designed to be manageable, effective, and long-lasting in classroom implementation.

TAG Protocol – A peer feedback process where students Tell a partner what they did well, Ask a question, and Give a suggestion for improvement.

Index

agreements, in 4 A's Protocol, 56
arguments, in 4 A's Protocol, 56
aspirations, in 4 A's Protocol, 56
Assessment Scramble strategy, 28–29
assumptions, in 4 A's Protocol, 56

Brooks, David, 2

choice, as deliberate, 4
Clues Approach protocol, 26–27
Comparing Work Samples, 36, 42–43
Compass Points routine, 34–35
consistency and precision, 3, 81–82

dashboard, elements of, 16–17
deep learning, 6, 7–8
Deep Learning Workshops phase
    In2Out Protocol, 64–65
    overview, 11-12, 13-14, 50-51
    Four A's Protocol, 49, 56–57
    Frayer Model, 49, 60–61
    SPAR (Spontaneous Argumentation) workshop, 49, 58–59
    2 Box Induction, 49, 54–55
    Venn Diagram tool, 51, 54–55
direct instruction, lecture compared, 1
direct modeling. *See* Surface Workshops phase
dispositional learning, defined, 6
dispositional strategies, as universal, 7
dispositional zone, 7

five guiding principles, 15
Four A's Protocol, 49, 56–57
four-square, elements of, 17–18
Frayer Model, 49, 60–61
Friendly Controversy, 64, 74–75

Gallery Walk, 64, 76–77
Guided Practice strategy, 44–45

habits
    overview, 5–6
    habit mapping, 8–10
    habit placement, 6–8
    in rigorous project-based learning, 11–14
Hattie, John, 3

I Describe, You Draw strategy, 36, 48–49
In2Out Protocol, 64–65
instructional routines, list of, 9, 13–14

Jigsaw strategy, 64, 68–69

Know/Need to Know process, 28, 30–31

late bloomers, 2
lecture, direct instruction compared, 1

marginal gains. *See* nuance
Matrix Problems protocol, 24–25
metacognition, 12

Need It, See It, Start It, Show It framework, 18–19
Need to Know (NTK), 28, 30–31
novelty versus nuance, 2
nuance, 1–4, 79–80
Numberless/Slow Reveal activity, 36, 46–47

Phase 1. *See* Project Launch phase
Phase 2. *See* Surface Workshops phase
Phase 3. *See* Deep Learning Workshops phase
Phase 4. *See* Project Conclusion/Reflection phase
precision and consistency, 3, 81–82
proactive versus reactive, 10
problem- and project-based learning (PBL), 2
professional learning communities (PLCs), 18–19
Progress and Proficiency Framework, 8, 10
Project Conclusion/Reflection phase
    overview, 12, 13–14, 64–65
    Friendly Controversy, 66, 74–75
    Gallery Walk, 64, 76–77
    Jigsaw strategy, 64, 68–69
    Red Team, 64, 70–71
    Situation Room strategy, 64, 72–73
    3 C's transfer workshop, 66–67
Project Launch phase
    overview, 11, 13–14, 22–23
    Assessment Scramble strategy, 28–29
    Clues Approach protocol, 26–27
    Compass Points routine, 34–35
    Know/Need to Know process, 28, 30–31
    Matrix Problems protocol, 24–25
    To and Through Strategy, 32–33

reactive versus proactive, 10
Red Team, 66, 72–74
reflection phase. *See* Project Conclusion/Reflection phase

respectful disagreement, 76
rigorous project-based learning (RPBL), 11–14. *See also* Deep Learning Workshops phase; Project Conclusion/Reflection phase; Project Launch phase; Surface Workshops phase
Rosenshine, B., 4

Search and Unseen Questions strategy, 36, 40–41
Situation Room strategy, 64, 72-73
SPAR (Spontaneous Argumentation) workshop, 49, 58–59
strategies, list of, 9, 13–14
surface learning, 6, 7–8
Surface Workshops phase
    overview, 11, 13–14, 36–37
    Comparing Work Samples, 36, 42–43
    Guided Practice strategy, 44–45
    I Describe, You Draw, 36, 48–50
    Numberless/Slow Reveal, 46–47
    Numberless/Slow Reveal activity, 36
    Search and Unseen Questions strategy, 36, 40–41
    Zoom In, Zoom Out process, 36, 38–39

3 C's transfer workshop, 66–67
3 Read method, 46–47
Through, defined, 32
To and Through Strategy, 32–33
transfer learning, 6, 7–8, 12
2 Box Induction, 50, 54–55

Venn Diagram tool, 49, 52–53
visual guides, use of, 16–19

"You Might be a Late Bloomer" (Brooks), 2

Zoom In, Zoom Out process, 36, 38–39

Join Our Impact Team Community

Join our learner-centered PLC community where we put students in the driver's seat!

Let's create schools that work for all of us!

Build multigenerational partnerships with **YES!** (Youth Equity Stewardship).

Competency Over Conformity

Embrace the power of personalized learning and unlock your potential with Competency-Based Learning.

Literacy and Justice for All

Discover the power of a comprehensive, research-based literacy education that meets the needs of every student.

Thank you!

Mimi & Todd Press exclusively publishes authors who are dedicated to making an impact through their work. By purchasing, reading and implementing their ideas, you deepen the impact and increase awareness for future learning.

More from Mimi & Todd Press:

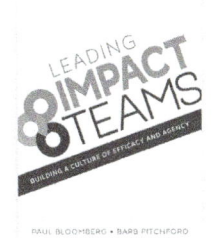

Leading Impact Teams: Building a Culture of Efficacy and Agency

Paul Bloomberg and Barb Pitchford

Re-Envisioning Rigor Books 1, 2 and 3

Michael McDowell and Aaron Eisberg

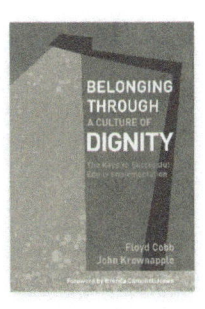

Belonging Through a Culture of Dignity: The Keys to Successful Equity Implementation

Floyd Cobb and John Krownapple

The Project Habit: Making Rigorous PBL Doable

Michael McDowell and Kelley S. Miller

Amplify Learner Voice through Culturally Responsive and Sustaining Assessment

Paul Bloomberg, Kara Vandas, Ingrid Twyman, et al.

Peer Power: Unite, Learn and Prosper: Activate an Assessment Revolution

Paul Bloomberg, Barb Pitchford, Kara Vandas, et al.

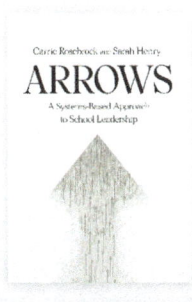

Arrows: A Systems-Based Approach to School Leadership

Carrie Rosebrock and Sarah Henry

Learner Agency: A Field Guide for Taking Flight

Kara Vandas, Jeanette Westfall, and Ashley Duvall

MIMI & TODD PRESS

mimitoddpress.com

Mimi & Todd Press discovers and publishes purpose-driven thought leaders who are striving to make a difference in the world. Visit us online to browse our catalogue of books and learn more.

Made in the USA
Monee, IL
30 June 2025